MICROFORM MARKET PLACE 1978-1979

MICROFORM MARKET PLACE 1978-1979

An International Directory
of Micropublishing

Edited by
Jeanne Short

Microform Review Inc.
520 Riverside Ave., Westport, CT 06880

Published by Microform Review Inc.
520 Riverside Ave.
P.O. Box 405 Saugatuck Station
Westport, Connecticut 06880

Cataloging in Publication Data

Microform Market Place.
  1978-1979
  1. Micropublishing-Directories
  I. Short, Jeanne
338.4'7'07057   Z286.M5

Library of Congress Catalog Card number 74-4811
ISBN 0-913672-22-X (Microform Review edition)
ISBN 0-7201-0803-9 (Mansell edition)

Printed and bound in the United States of America

MICROFORM
MARKET PLACE
1978-1979

Contents

Introduction

Microform Market Place provides comprehensive information about micropublishers under one cover so that microform purchasers can have easier access to this specialized group of publishers.

MMP contains nine sections: Directory of Micropublishers; Reprographic Centers; Subject Index (Micropublishers are listed under subjects in which they offer micropublications); Geographic Index; Mergers and Acquisitions; Organizations involved with Micrographics Education; Bibliography of Primary Sources; Calendar 1978-1979; and a Names and Numbers Directory.

MMP does not include micrographics equipment and supply manufacturers. This area is well covered by several publications offered by the National Micrographics Association (NMA), 8728 Colesville Rd., Silver Spring, MD 20910.

The editor welcomes suggestions for improving future editions of *MMP* and reminds users that the next edition will be published June, 1980.

Jeanne Short

Section I

DIRECTORY OF MICROPUBLISHERS

This section provides information on micropublishing organizations (both commercial and non-commercial) throughout the world. The term micropublisher has been broadly defined as follows: An organization that markets micropublished information. Parts catalog micropublishers or publishers of newspapers and periodicals whose respective publications are sold in microform by another company (e.g. *Time* magazine) are not included. Organizations that merely offer reprographic services on request are listed in Section II. All entries are arranged alphabetically word by word. Abbreviations and acronyms are entered alphabetically as they are spelled.

ACADEMIC MICROFORMS INC.
1317 Filbert St., Philadelphia, PA 19107

Tel: 215/563-4040
Microformats offered: microfiche; 35mm microfilm
Micropublication programs: Academic publications in series, scholarly periodicals and selected archival collections.

ACADEMIC PRESS, INC., A Subsidiary of Harcourt Brace Jovanovich, Publishers
111 Fifth Ave., New York, NY 10003

Tel: 212/741-6800
Senior Vice President: Robert L. Biewen
Microformats offered: microfiche
Micropublication programs: Micropublishes library editions and journals.

A.C.R.P.P.

See: Association pour la Conservation et la Reproduction Photographique de la Presse

AESTHETIC, RECONSTRUCTIVE, AND FACIAL PLASTIC SURGERY
(An International Microform Journal), 16 Prescott St., Brookline, MA 02146

Tel: 617/566-2050
Editor-in-Chief: Richard C. Webster, M.D.
Microformats offered: color microfiche
Micropublication programs: Micropublication and distribution of longer articles
 (in color) than can be published economically with standard techniques.
 Topics are integral to cosmetic and functional plastic surgery.

AFRICAN IMPRINT LIBRARY SERVICES
Guard Hill Rd., Bedford, NY 10506

Tel: 914/234-3752
Director: Allen R. Boyd
Microformats offered: microfiche; 35mm microfilm
Micropublication programs: Production and distribution of microforms of
 African publications, especially newspapers.

ALLERTON PRESS, INC.
150 Fifth Ave., New York,NY 10011

Tel: 212/924-3950
Editor: Edward Michaels
Microformats offered: 35mm microfilm
Micropublication programs: Applied Solar Energy (cover-to-cover English
 translation of Geliotekhnika).

AMERICAN ASSOCIATION FOR THE ADVANCEMENT OF SCIENCE
 (AAAS)
1515 Massachusetts Ave., N.W., Washington, DC 20005

Tel: 202/467-4400
Audio Tape Dept.: Michael Van Meter
Microform Clerk: Kathy Springer
Microform Clerk: Susan Stinchcomb
Microformats offered: 35mm microfilm
Micropublication programs: Scientific periodicals and symposia offered on
 microfilm.

AMERICAN ASTRONAUTICAL SOCIETY
P.O. Box 28130, San Diego, CA 92128

Tel: 714/746-4005; 714/487-7560
Manager, Publications Office: Dr. H. Jacobs
Microformats offered: microfiche; 35mm microfilm
Micropublication programs: Publishes on microfiche AAS Proceedings and
  supplements thereto that do not appear in hard copy; out of print AAS books
  and the *Journal of the Astronautical Sciences*.

AMERICAN CHEMICAL SOCIETY
Microform Program, 1155 Sixteenth St., N.W., Washington, DC 20036

Tel: 202/872-4600
Telex: 892582
Cable Address: jiechem
Executive Director: Dr. Raymond P. Mariella
Manager, Microforms and Back Issues: Caroline M. Grills
Microformats offered: microfiche; 16mm and 35mm microfilm
Micropublication programs: Micropublishes 20 scientific periodicals on
  microfiche simultaneously with the paper edition. Backfiles date from 1974
  on microfiche and from the first issue of each publication on microfilm.

AMERICAN CONCRETE INSTITUTE
P.O.Box 19150 Redford Station, 22400 W. Seven Mile Rd., Detroit, MI 48219

Tel: 313/532-2600
Journal Sales: Howard McFarland
Microformats offered: microfiche
Micropublication programs: Journal of the American Concrete Institute and
  Concrete Abstracts.

AMERICAN INSTITUTE OF AERONAUTICS AND ASTRONAUTICS, INC.
750 Third Avenue, New York, NY 10017

Tel: 212/867-8300
Microformats offered: microfiche
Micropublication programs: All meeting papers of the AIAA and International
  Aerospace Abstracts.

AMERICAN INSTITUTE OF PHYSICS
335 East 45th St., New York, NY 10017

Tel: 212/661-9404
Manager, Marketing Services: David R. Dresia
Manager, Back Numbers, Microfilm: Charles Lehanka
Microformats offered: microfiche; 16mm and 35mm microfilm
Micropublication programs: Microform editions of publications of the American Institute of Physics and The Institute of Physics (U.K.). Emphasis is on physics and related topics.

AMERICAN JEWISH PERIODICAL CENTER, HEBREW UNION COLLEGE
Jewish Institute of Religion, 3101 Clifton Ave., Cincinnati, OH 45220

Tel: 513/221-1875
Director: Herbert Zafren
Microformats offered: 35mm microfilm
Micropublication programs: Jewish periodicals.

AMERICAN LIBRARY ASSOCIATION
50 East Huron St., Chicago, IL 60611

Tel: 312/994-6780
Editor: Howard S. White
Microformats offered: microfiche
Micropublication programs: The Sourcebook of Library Technology (a cumulative edition of Library Technology Reports, 1965-1977).

AMERICAN THEOLOGICAL LIBRARY ASSOCIATION BOARD OF MICROTEXT
Princeton Theological Seminary, Speer Library, P.O. Box 111, Princeton, NJ 08540

Tel: 609/921-8300
Executive Secretary: Charles Willard
Microformats offered: microfiche; 35mm reel microfilm
Micropublication programs: Nineteenth century church periodicals; scholarly periodicals in religion; theses; manuscripts and monographs.

AMERICANA UNLIMITED
P.O. Box 50447, 1701 North 11th Avenue, Tucson, AZ 85703

Tel: 602/792-3453
President: Gordon L. Cox
General Sales Manager & Vice-President: John D. Gilchriese
Promotional Manager: Ernest Hoffman
Customer Service: Dianne E. Ward
Microformats offered: 35mm microfilm
Micropublication programs: Regional, state, county and local histories of the
    United States including Alaska and Hawaii; military history and Canadiana;
    telephone directories through 1942; city directories of major American cities
    from the mid-19th century through World War II.

AMS PRESS, INC.
56 East 13th St., New York, NY 10003

Tel: 212/777-4700
Cable Address: abmagserv
Manager-Microfilm Division: Joseph Scarpulla
Microformats offered: microfiche; 35mm microfilm
Micropublication programs: Classic Bibliographies and Library Reference
    Works: Little Literary Magazines on Microfilm; Comics on Microfilm;
    International Peace Relations; Marquis Who's Who; U.S. Temporary
    National Economic Committee: Investigation of Concentration of Economic
    Power; Federal Writers Project.

ANDRONICUS PUBLISHING COMPANY, INC.
666 Fifth Ave., New York, NY 10019

Tel: 212/245-8498
President: John Haldi
Editor: Hermine M. Watterson
Microformats offered: microfiche; 35mm microfilm
Micropublication programs: African Studies Program; Group Tensions in
    America; League of Nations Mandate Reports; British Colonial Reports.

ANTIQUARIAN AND LANDMARKS SOCIETY, INC.
394 Main Street, Hartford, CT 06103

Tel: 203/247-8996
Microformats offered: 35mm microfilm
Micropublication programs: The Social Reform Papers of John James
   McCook.

THE ARCHITECTURAL PRESS LTD.
9 Queen Annes Gate, London SW1H 9BY England

Tel: 01-930-0611
Cable Address: Buildable: London
Directors: J.M. Regan, J. Hastings
Director (books and microfiche): G. Golzen
Sales (books and microfiche): A.J. Mason
Microformats offered: microfiche
Micropublication programs: Microfiche copies of out-of-print books and
   current academic working papers on architecture and related fields.

ARCHIVES CANADA MICROFICHES
   Picture Division, Public Archives of Canada, 395 Wellington Street, Ottawa,
   Ontario, K1A ON3 Canada

Tel: 613/995-1300
Division Chief: Georges Delisle
General Editor: Douglas Schoenherr
Microformats offered: microfiche (color)
Micropublication programs: Documentary, historical art from the Public
   Archives of Canada's collections on color microfiche; each fiche
   accompanied by printed descriptive catalogue with artist's biography and
   references.

ASIA LIBRARY SERVICES
P.O. Box C, Auburn, NY 13021

Microformats offered: 35mm microfilm
Micropublication programs: Micropublication of research materials
   (newspapers, news magazines, press summaries, journals, etc.) on
   Thailand and Laos. Languages include: English, Thai, French, Chinese,
   and Lao.

ASSOCIATION FOR COMPUTATIONAL LINGUISTICS
c/o Dr. D.E. Walker, Secretary-Treasurer, SR1 International, Menlo Park, CA
  94025
President: Jonathan Allen
Managing Editor: Donald E. Walker
Editor: David G. Hays
Microformats offered: microfiche
Micropublication programs: Publication of a professional journal covering the
  field of computational linguistics; it includes original articles, reviews,
  surveys, announcements, and a comprehensive bibliography of current
  research.

ASSOCIATION POUR LA CONSERVATION ET LA REPRODUCTION
  PHOTOGRAPHIQUE DE LA PRESSE (A.C.R.P.P.)
4 rue Louvois, 75002 Paris, France

Tel: 742-51-48
Microformats offered: 16mm and 35mm microfilm
Micropublication programs: Microfilming of French newspapers.

AUDIR
See: Fondation Nationale des Sciences Politiques

L'AVANT—SCÈNE
27, rue Saint-André-des-Arts, 75006 Paris, France

Tel: 325-52-29
Publisher: Jacques Charrière
U.S. Representative: William Gilcher, 107 West Lewis Street, Ithaca, NY
  14850
Microformats offered: microfiche
Micropublication programs: La Revue internationale d'histoire du cinéma,
  published quarterly on microfiche. Editor-in-chief: Vincent Pinel.

BELL & HOWELL MICRO PHOTO DIVISION
Old Mansfield Rd., Wooster, OH 44691

Tel: 216/264-6666
Telex: 98-6496
President: John C. Marken
Manager, Publication Products: Dwain Pearce
Manager, Advertising and Sales Promotion: Russell H. Zeskey
Microformats offered: microfiche; 16mm and 35mm reel microfilm
Micropublication programs: Micropublisher of over 3,000 newspapers on
    microfilm and indexer of several major dailies; over 400 popular periodicals
    on microfiche, and numerous special collections (e.g. Telephone
    Directories on microfiche).

BERANDOL MUSIC LIMITED
11 St. Joseph St., Toronto, Ontario, M4Y 1J8 Canada

Tel: 416/924-8121
President: Ralph Cruickshank
Microformats offered: microfiche
Micropublication programs: MUSIcache, a basic music library of standard
    repertoire is available from Bell and Howell.

BIBLIOTHÈQUE NATIONALE DU QUÉBEC,
    Service de microphotographie
1700, rue Saint-Denis, Montréal, Québec, Canada H2X 3K6

Tel: 514/670-3470
Telex: 055-61294
Head of the Dept.: Réjean Savard
Microformats offered: microfiche; 16mm and 35mm microfilm
Micropublication programs: Microfilming rare books, serials, and geographical
    maps edited in Québec or related to Québec; direct micropublishing of
    current events files and research works form the Bibliothèque nationale du
    Québec.

BIOSCIENCES INFORMATION SERVICE
2100 Arch St., Philadelphia, PA 19103

Tel: 215/LO-8-4016
Executive Director: Dr. H.E. Kennedy
Director for Professional Services: A.W. Elias
Director for Research and Development: J.R. Smith
Director for Scientific Affairs: R. Marchisotto
Microformats offered: microfiche; 16mm reel microfilm
Micropublication programs: Biological Abstracts and Cumulative Indexes
    available on microfilm 1927-present, on microfiche 1970-1974.

BLACKWELL BIBLIOGRAPHICAL SERVICES LIMITED
P.O.Box 72, Oxford, OX1 2EY England

Tel: Oxford, England (0865) 49111, ext. 68
Telex: 837512
Chairman: Julian Blackwell
Managing Director: Nigel S.M. Cox
Editorial: Clement Jewitt
Microformats offered: microfiche
Micropublication programs: Forthcoming Books Service, a monthly pre-
    publication book announcement service.

BLOCH AND COMPANY
P.O. Box 77, Fairfax Station, VA 22039

Director: Louis M. Bloch, Jr.
Microformats offered: microfiche
Micropublication programs: The name index and abstract of the Fairfax
    County, Virginia Court records from 1749-1774.

BRITISH LIBRARY. BIBLIOGRAPHIC SERVICES DIVISION
Store St., London WC1E 7DG England

Tel: (01) 636-1544
Telex: 22787
Director General: Richard Coward
Microformats offered: ultramicrofiche
Micropublication programs: Books in English, an English language
    bibliography combining British National Bibliography and Library of
    Congress records and author/title sequence. Bimonthly progressive
    cumulations on ultramicrofiche.

BROOKHAVEN PRESS, a Division of Northern Engraving Company
901 26th Street NW, Washington, DC 20037

Tel: 202/338-8870
Order Processing Dept.: P.O. Box 1653, La Crosse, WI 54601
Tel: 608/782-4180
Publisher: Albert Diaz
Microformats offered: microfiche; 16mm and 35mm microfilm
Micropublication programs: Microform reprints, in all subject fields, of journals,
    government documents, archival collections, multi-volume sets, and other
    materials used for scholarly research.

BUFFALO AND ERIE COUNTY HISTORICAL SOCIETY
25 Nottingham Court, Buffalo, NY 14216
Tel: 716/873-9644
Associate Director: Lester W. Smith
Curator for Manuscripts: Arthur C. Detmers
Microformats offered: 35mm microfilm
Micropublication programs: Millard Fillmore Papers.

ALVINA TREUT BURROWS INSTITUTE, INC.
Box 49, Manhasset, NY 11030

Tel: 516/869-8457
Executive Secretary: Dolly Svobodny
Microformats offered: microfiche
Micropublication programs: Specialized collections dealing with research and
  experimental programs in language arts and the teaching of reading;
  collections dealing with the teaching of language arts, English and American
  literature, and curriculum design on language arts and reading.

BUTTERWORTHS PTY LTD.
586 Pacific Hwy. Chatswood N.S.W. 2067 Australia

Tel: 02-412-3444
Telex: AA 22033
Cable Address: Butterwort Australia
Microform Division Manager: C.J. Wood
Microformats offered: microfiche; 16mm and 35mm microfilm
Micropublication programs: Argus Law Reports (1895-1973); Gazette Law
  Reports of New Zealand (1898-1952); New South Wales Reports (1960-
  1970); Hong Kong Law reports (1905-1956); Commonwealth Arbitration
  Reports (1905-present); Australian Law Theses and Law Seminar Papers
  (1960-present); Criminology-Australian Newspaper Cuttings File (hard
  copy indexed).

CALIFORNIA STATE LIBRARY
P.O.Box 2037, Sacramento, CA 95809

Tel: 916/445-5156
Director: Ethel S. Crockett
Microformats offered: microfiche
Micropublication programs: California Union List of Periodicals.

CANADIAN LIBRARY ASSOCIATION
151 Sparks St., Ottawa, Ontario, Canada KIP 5E3

Tel: 613/232-9625
Chairman: Edward Phelps
Microformats offered: 35mm microfilm
Micropublication programs: Canadian newspapers (1752-1954), periodicals, journals, studies, official gazettes and provincial government documents.

J.S. CANNER & COMPANY
49-65 Lansdowne St., Boston, MA 02215

Tel: 617/261-8600
Cable Address: CANNBOOKS BOSTON
General Manager: Marshall Lebowitz
Microformats offered: microcards
Micropublication programs: Microcard reprints of a variety of scholarly journals.

CARFAX PUBLISHING COMPANY
Haddon House, Dorchester-on-Thames, Oxford 0X9 8JZ, England

Directors: Roger Osborn-King and Duncan Spence
Microformats offered: microfiche
Micropublication programs: All of Carfax's journals are available in microfiche. Two are microfiche-only journals: CORE (Collected Original Resources in Education) and Journal of Sources in Educational History.

CARIBBEAN IMPRINT LIBRARY SERVICES
Guard Hill Rd., Bedford, NY 10506

Tel: 914/234-3752
Microformats offered: microfiche; 35mm microfilm
Micropublication programs: Production and distribution of microforms of Caribbean publications, especially newspapers.

THE CARROLLTON PRESS
1911 Fort Myer Drive, #905, Arlington, VA 22209

Tel: 703/525-5940
Cable Address: Caropress
President: William W. Buchanan
Library Services Manager: Mary Tisdale
Direct Mail Advertising Manager: James S. McGreevy
Foreign Office: 24 Hamilton Street, Inverness, Scotland
Manager: William Rae
Microformats offered: microfiche, 16mm and 35mm microfilm
Micropublication programs: The Declassified Documents Reference System
    (abstracts and indexes in book format plus full text of documents on fiche)
    and U.S. Government Bibliography Masterfile, 1924-1974.

THE CATHOLIC UNIVERSITY OF AMERICA PRESS, INC.
620 Michigan Ave., N.E., Washington, DC 20064

Tel: 202/635-5052
Manager: Marian E. Goode
Microformats offered: 35mm microfilm
Micropublication programs: The American Catholic Directories; Sadlier
    Directories; Hoffman Directories

CENTER FOR CHINESE RESEARCH MATERIALS, Association of Research
    Libraries
1527 New Hampshire Ave., N.W., Washington, DC 20036

Tel: 202/387-7172
Director: Ping-kuen Yu
Microformats offered: 35mm microfilm
Micropublication programs: Microfilm of runs of Chinese-language
    newspapers, periodicals, gazettes and monographs.

CENTER FOR RESEARCH LIBRARIES
5721 South Cottage Grove, Chicago, IL 60637

Tel: 312/955-4545
Microform Director: Ray Boylan
Microformats offered: 35mm microfilm
Micropublication programs: The Center for Research Libraries is a not for profit library supported by 104 research libraries in North America. As part of its program it microfilms rarely held research materials. Most of the filming is done by special projects which are supported by subscribing institutions.

CENTRAL ASIAN RESEARCH CENTRE, LTD.
1B Parkfield St., London, N1 OPR England

Tel: 01-226-5371
Director: David L. Morison
Secretary: Margery Geoghegan
Microformats offered: 35mm microfilm
Micropublication programs: Central Asian Review.

CENTRE DE PREPARATION DOCUMENTAIRE À LA TRADUCTION
16 rue Beaurepaire, 75010 Paris, France

President: Gérard Pierson
Microformats offered: microfiche
Micropublication programs: Current Terminology Awareness Bulletin and Langue Chinoise/Chinese Language.

THE CENTRE FOR EAST ASIAN CULTURAL STUDIES
c/o The Toyo Bunko (Oriental Library), Honkomagome 2-chome, 28-21, Bunkyo-ku Tokyo, 113, Japan

Tel: 03-942-0121
Cable Address: Toyobunko, Tokyo
Chief, Research and Documentation Section: Shigeru Ikuta
Microformats offered: 35mm microfilm
Micropublication programs: Southeast Asian materials.

CHADWYCK-HEALEY LTD.
20 Newmarket Road, Cambridge, England

Tel: 0223 311479
Managing Director: Charles Chadwyck-Healey
Microformats offered: microfiche (including color); 35mm reel microfilm (including color)
Micropublication programs: Art exhibition catalogs on microfiche, European and World official statistical serials on microfiche, Archives of British and American publishers on microfiche, BBC daily radio news on microfiche, government publications on microform, Index of American Design on color microfiche.
North American distributor: see Somerset House

CHAPMAN & HALL LTD.
Northway, Andover, Hampshire SP 105BE England

Tel: Andover (0264) 62141
Telex: 47214
Marketing Director: H.J. von Knorring
Deputy Marketing Manager: Lyndsay Williams
Microformats offered: microfiche
Micropublication programs: Reproduction of out-of-print books.

CHEMICAL ABSTRACTS SERVICE, A division of the American Chemical Society
The Ohio State University, Columbus, OH 43210

Tel: 614/421-6940
Microformats offered: microfiche
Micropublication programs: The International CODEN Directory is a comprehensive index to all CODEN assigned since the introduction of CODEN in 1954.

THE CHEMICAL SOCIETY
Burlington House, London W1V OBN, England

Tel: 01-734-9864
Telex: 268001
Asst. Director of Publications: Dr. Ivor A. Williams
Microformats offered: microfiche
Micropublication programs: Journal of Chemical Research is the first pure-
chemistry journal to be published according to the synopsis/microform
method.

CHILTON BOOK COMPANY
Radner, PA 19089

Tel: 215/687-8200
Sales Representative: Martha Kemplin
Microformats offered: microfiche
Micropublication programs: Chilton's Motor/Age Professional Automotive
Service Manual 1977 and Chilton's Motor/Age Professional Labor Guide
and Parts Manual 1977.

THE CHURCH OF JESUS CHRIST OF LATTER-DAY SAINTS
Historical Department, East Wing, 50 East North Temple Street, Salt Lake
City, UT 84150

Tel: 801/531-2745
Editor: Melvin L. Bashore
Microformats offered: microfiche
Micropublication programs: Index to Mormonism in Periodical literature is
issued annually.

CLEARWATER PUBLISHING COMPANY, INC.
1995 Broadway, Room 401, New York, NY 10023

Tel: 212/873-2100
Telex: 237334
President: Norman A. Ross
Customer Service: Maureen Grice
Canadian Office: 231 Hollyberry Trail, Willowdale , Ontario, Canada M2H 2P3
Tel: 416/494-6143
Director: Dr. Lewis J. Rosen
Microformats offered: microfiche; 35mm microfilm
Micropublication programs: Micropublisher of the Library of American Indian
    Affairs (primarily documents of the Indian Claims Commission and
    American Indian periodicals) and the Library of World Peace Studies
    (primarily periodicals and the card catalogs of major peace libraries, e.g.,
    The Peace Palace library at The Hague). Clearwater is the appointed
    U.S.-Canadian distributor for many European micropublishers.

COMMERCE CLEARING HOUSE, INC.
4025 W. Peterson Ave., Chicago, IL 60646

Tel: 312/CO-7-9010
President: Robert C. Bartlett
Managing Editor: Allen Schechter
Microform Activities Manager: Charles V. R. Edward
Microformats offered: microfiche (including ultrafiche); 16mm and 35mm
    microfilm
Micropublication programs: Micropublication of Securities and Exchange
    Commission background decisions and rulings as well as current rulings
    relating to taxes and SEC matters.

COMMONWEALTH MICROFILM LIBRARY
7502 Bath Rd., Mississauga, Ontario, Canada L4T 1L2

Tel: 416/677-0697
TWX: 610-492-9473
Marketing Director: Lorne C. Mann
Microformats offered: microfiche; 35mm microfilm
Micropublication programs: Archival materials such as: newspapers,
    periodicals and out-of-print books. Current materials including newspapers,
    periodicals and government documents.

COMPUTER SCIENCE PRESS, INC.
9125 Fall River Lane, Potomac, MD 20854

Tel: 301/299-2040
Microformats offered: microfiche
Micropublication programs: Micropublication of books in Computer Chess
    Series, Computer Software Engineering Series, Digital System Design
    Series and Journal of Design Automation & Fault Tolerant Computing.

CONGRESSIONAL DIGEST CORPORATION
3231 P Street N.W., Washington, DC 20007

Tel: 202/333-7332
President: A. Gram Robinson
Publisher: T. N. Robinson III
Editor: John E. Shields
Microformats offered: microfiche; 16mm and 35mm microfilm
Micropublication programs: Complete positive film backfile of Digest, 1921 to
    date available in microfiche and microfilm. It is internally indexed by volume,
    with a separate set of annual indexes available.

CONGRESSIONAL INFORMATION SERVICE, INC.
7101 Wisconsin Ave., Washington, DC 20014

Tel: 301/654-1550
President: James B. Adler
Micropublishing Director: Jeffrey Heynen
Public Relations Director: Howard Goldstein
National Sales Manager: John P. Beil
Microformats offered: microfiche; 35mm microfilm
Micropublication programs: CIS is a commercial indexer and micropublisher of
    Federal, state and foreign government documents.

CONGRESSIONAL QUARTERLY
1414 22nd St., N.W., Washington, DC 20037

Tel: 202/296-6800
Research Director: Robert Cuthriell
Sales Manager: Robert C. Hur
Microformats offered: microfiche; 16mm microfilm
Micropublication programs: Complete Congressional Voting Records.

CONSUMERS' ASSOCIATION
14 Buckingham Street, London WC2N 6DS England

Tel: 01-839-1222
Telex: 918197
Director: Peter Goldman
Chief Librarian: Peter Thomas
Microformats offered: microfiche
Micropublication programs: Consumer magazines Which? 1957-; Motoring
    Which? 1962-; Money Which? 1968-; Handyman Which? 1971-; Holiday
    Which? 1974-; British local consumer group magazines; Local Authority;
    Consumer Protection Annual Reports.

CORNELL UNIVERSITY DEPARTMENT OF MANUSCRIPTS UNIVERSITY
    ARCHIVES
John M. Olin Research Library, Ithaca, NY 14850

Tel: 607/256-3530
Archivist: Gould P. Colman
Microformats offered: 35mm microfilm
Micropublication programs: George Bancroft Papers: Andrew Dickson White
    Papers: Goldwin Smith Papers: Charles Abrams Papers: Willard Straight
    Papers, Emily Howland Papers.

CREATIVE MICROLIBRARIES, INC., A division of Svobodny Development
    Corporation
Box 49, Manhasset, NY 11030

Tel: 516/869-8457
President: Dolly Svobodny
Microformats offered: microfiche
Micropublication programs: Creative MicroLibraries publishes specialized
    collections of current interest, particularly research materials on current
    affairs, political science, civics, government and world history.

DAKOTA GRAPHICS, INC.
9655 W. Colfax Ave., Denver, CO 80215

Tel: 303/237-0408
Exec. Vice President: John DeAngelis
Vice President: Dean Ward
Microformats offered: 35mm microfilm
Micropublication programs: German musicological periodicals.

DARTMOUTH COLLEGE LIBRARY
Baker Library, Hanover, NH 03755

Tel: 603/646-2235
Microformats offered: microfiche
Micropublication programs: Grenville Clark Papers and A Microfiche Catalog
of the Library of Jeremiah Smith.

DATA COURIER, INC.
620 South Fifth Street, Louisville, KY 40202

Tel: 502/582-4111
Microformats offered: microfiche
Micropublication programs: Back issues of Oceanic Abstracts and Pollution
Abstracts.

DATAFLOW SYSTEMS, INC.
7758 Wisconsin Ave., Bethesda, MD 20014

Tel: 301/654-9133
President: B. Doudnikoff
Vice President: J.B. Malcom
Vice President Sales: R.R. Stine
Treasurer: V. From
Microformats offered: microfiche; 35mm microfilm
Micropublication programs: Systems offered in the following areas: U.S. and
Canadian Medical School catalogs on microfiche, major U.S. university
catalogs on 35mm microfilm, energy documents on microfiche, etc.
Dataflow also offers micrographic consulting services.

DATAMICS
120 Liberty St., New York, NY 10006

Microformats offered: 16mm and 35mm microfilm
Micropublication programs: Government documents and history.

WM. DAWSON & SONS LTD.
Cannon House, Folkestone, Kent CT19 5EE England

Tel: Folkestone 57421
Telex: 96392
Cable Address: Dawbooks Folkestone
Managing Director: G. Krayenbrink
Mgr. Microfiche Division: G. Harland
Microformats offered: microfiche
Micropublication programs: Science and humanities periodicals.

DISCLOSURE INCORPORATED
4827 Rugby Avenue, Bethesda, MD 20014

Tel: 301/931-0100
President: Philip E. Hixon
Marketing Vice-President: Steven Goldspiel
Controller: Ralph Silware
Executive Vice-President: Robert N. Snyder
Microformats offered: microfiche (including color); 16mm and 35mm microfilm
    (including color)
Micropublication programs: Publishes all Securities and Exchange
Commission public filings on microfiche. Contracts micrographic services,
including indexing.

THE DUNLAP SOCIETY
Visual Documentation Program, Box 297, Essex, NY 12936

Tel: 518/963-7373
Executive Secretary: Isabel Barrett Lowry
Administrative Assistant: Norma C. Jackson
Microformats offered: microfiche
Micropublication programs: Original publications of visual material covering a
    wide range of topics in American art. Comprehensive text appears as
    captions on the microfiche.

EDINBURGH UNIVERSITY PRESS
22 George Square, Edinburgh EH8 9LF, Scotland

Tel: 031-667-1011
Cable Address: Edinpress
Press Secretary: Archie Turnbull
Production Manager: John McI. Davidson
Sales Manager: Gordon Angus
Microformats offered: microfiche (including color)
Micropublication programs: Colour microfiche of illustrations included as part
   of conventional book (Talbot Rice & Gray: *The Illustrations to the World
   History of Rashid al-Din*).

EDUCATIONAL INFORMATION SERVICES, INC.
Air Rights Bldg., P.O. Box 5826, Washington, DC 20014

Tel: 301/770-6440
President: James J. Prevel
Microformats offered: microfiche
Micropublication programs: Education Information Collection Television.

EDUCATIONAL RESOURCES INFORMATION CENTER (ERIC)
Sponsored by the National Institute of Education, Office of Dissemination and
   Resources, Washington, DC 20208

Tel: 202/254-5555
Chief: Charles Hoover
Microformats offered: microfiche
Micropublication programs: Educational Resources Information Center
   (ERIC) makes available through hundreds of libraries and information
   centers over 100,000 unpublished, hard to find documents on all phases,
   levels and subject areas of education.

EDUCATIONAL TESTING SERVICE
Princeton, NJ, 08540

Tel: 609/921-9000
Cable Address: EDUCTESTSVC
Head, Test Collection: Pamela Rosen
Microformats offered: microfiche
Micropublication programs: Tests in Microfiche, a collection of research
    devices.

ELSEVIER SEQUOIA S.A.
Avenue de la Gare 50, P.O. Box 851, 1001 Lausanne, Switzerland

Tel: (021) 20 7381
Microformats offered: 16mm and 35mm microfilm
Micropublication programs: Back volumes on microfilm of over 100 journals
    published by Elsevier Sequoia, Switzerland, Elsevier/North-Holland,
    Ireland and Elsevier Scientific and North-Holland Publishing Companies,
    Holland.

EMBRYO PUBLISHERS
17 Woodside Place, Glascow C3, Scotland

Tel: 041-332-1066
Microformats offered: microfiche
Micropublication programs: Scottish archives; out-of-print books and journals
    for specialists. Subject studies include The First Statistical Account of
    Scotland.

ENGINEERING INDEX, INC.
United Engineering Center, 345 E. 47th St., New York, NY 10017

Tel: 212/644-7600
Executive Director: John E. Creps, Jr.
Manager, Marketing Division: John H. Veyette Jr.
Microformats offered: 16mm and 35mm microfilm
Micropublication programs: The Engineering Index Annual and Alpha-Deka
    Microfile.

ENVIRONMENT INFORMATION CENTER
292 Madison Avenue, New York, NY 10017

Tel: 212/949-9494
Publisher: James Kollegger
Microformats offered: microfiche
Micropublication programs: Documents and periodicals on environmental topics are provided on microfiche for the Envirofiche System. Statefiche provides environmental laws for each state on microfiche.

EP MICROFORM LIMITED
Bradford Rd., East Ardsley, Wakefield, Yorkshire, WF3 2JN England

Tel: Wakefield 823971 (0924)
Telex: 917963 Solomon London
Cable Address: Edpro Wakefield
Managing Director: J.S. Lofthouse
Microformats offered: microfiche; 16mm and 35mm microfilm (including color)
Micropublication programs: Micropublishes over 5000 titles. Current major projects include: government publications relating to Africa, British records relating to America, British education reports, literary manuscripts, and Livery Company records.

EXCERPTA MEDICA
305 Keizersgracht, Amsterdam, The Netherlands

Tel: 020-644-38
Telex: 14664
Directors: Nico de Gier and Willem van Leeuwen
Vice President Marketing: Barrie Stern
Marketing and Promotion Manager: Arnold A.J. Jansen
Microformats offered: microfiche; 16mm and 35mm microfilm
Micropublication programs: Micropublishes all 49 sections of volumes on medical topics three years after printed publication.

FACTS ON FILE, INC., A subsidiary of Commerce Clearing House, Inc.
119 West 57th Street, New York, NY 10019

Tel: 212/CO-5-2011
Cable: Factsfile, New York
President: Howard M. Epstein
Vice-President: Edward Knappman
Business Manager/Circulation Manager: Henry Grant
Director of Marketing: Howard Langer
Customer Service: Senta Seda
Microformats offered: microfiche
Micropublication programs: Editorials on File is normally published twice a
    month as a compilation of editorials on issues in the news. The microfiche
    version comes out as an annual approximately a year after final publication.

FAIRCHILD MICROFILMS, VISUALS DIVISION, FAIRCHILD
    PUBLICATIONS, INC.
7 East 12th St., New York, NY 10003

Tel: 212/741-4067
Microformats offered: 35mm microfilm
Micropublication programs: Fairchild Microfilm micropublishes the Fairchild
    trade newspapers which include: Women's Wear Daily; Daily News Record;
    American Metal Market; Electronic News; Footwear News; Supermarket
    News; HFD/Retail Home Furnishings; Energy User News; W. Substantial
    back-file coverage is available.

THE FINANCIAL TIMES
Bracken House, Cannon St., London EC4P 4BY England

Tel: 01-248-8000
Telex: 8811506
Sales Manager: Beverly Pullen
Microformats offered: microfiche
Micropublication programs: MIRAC Service—a microfiche publication of
    report and accounts of all United Kingdom quoted companies, 1968 to date.

FONDATION NATIONALE DES SCIENCES POLITIQUES
27, rue Saint-Guillaume, 75341 Paris Cedex 07, France

Tel: 260-39-60

Microformats offered: microfiche

Micropublication programs: Bibliothèque de Recherche: Sciences humaines;
Recherches en Economic Appliquee; Structures Sociales sous l'Ancien
Régime; Recherches en Histoire Sociale; Histoire des Mentalités; Etudes
Africaines; La Société Espagnole a l'Époque Moderne; Études de
Sinologie.

THE FOUNDATION CENTER
888 Seventh Avenue, New York, NY 10019

Tel: 212/975-1120

President: Thomas R. Buckman

Treasurer: William Kirsch

Director, Library Services: Carol M. Kurzig

Microformats offered: microfiche

Micropublication programs: The Foundation Center issues two annual
microfiche series. Foundation Annual Reports on Microfiche—a set which
includes all published annual reports available from philanthropic
foundations, currently about 350-400. COMSEARCH Printouts—computer
printouts listing foundation grants in approximately 55 broad subject
categories.

FRANCE-EXPANSION
336-340 rue Saint Honore 75001 Paris, France

Tel: 260-32-09

Cable Address: Francexpansion, Paris

President: Jacques Dodeman

Microformats offered: microfiche

Micropublication programs: Archives de la Linguistique Française—French
language dictionaries and glossaries published between the 15th and the
19th centuries; Bulletin Signalétique du C.N.R.S.—Scientific abstracts;
Journal des Américanistes—All issues 1895-1972.

GAS CHROMATOGRAPHY SERVICE
Preston Technical Abstracts Co., 6366 Gross Point Road, P.O. Box 312, Niles, IL 60648

Microformats offered: 16mm and 35mm microfilm
Micropublication programs: Gas Chromatography Abstracts and Journal of Chromatographic Science.

GAYLORD BROS., INC.
P.O. Box 61, Syracuse, NY 13201

Tel: 315/457-5070
President: Walter W. Curley
Controller: Augustine J. Charles
General Sales Manager: Warren D. Ross
Promotion Manager: Erwin R. Vrooman
Customer Service: Anne Kincella
Microformats offered: microfiche
Micropublication programs: College Catalogs on Microfiche; National Union Catalog on Microfiche.

GENERAL MICROFILM COMPANY
10 Iman St., Cambridge, MA 02139

Tel: 617/864-2820
President: George M. Lexander
Vice President: John P. Eustis II
Special Projects Manager: Cheryl Copeland
Microformats offered: microfiche; 35mm microfilm
Micropublication programs: The scholarly micropublications emphasize literature, the humanities and government documents. Within these areas, there is a significant amount of pre-1800 literature in various languages.

GEORGIA INSTITUTE OF TECHNOLOGY
Georgia Tech Libraries, Georgia Institute of Technology, Atlanta, GA 30332

Tel: 404/894-4510
Director: Dr. Graham Roberts
Microformats offered: microfiche
Micropublication programs: Georgia Tech Library's Complete Card Catalog is
   published on microfiche. There is an annual reissue on COM in December,
   monthly COM supplements cumulated monthly and the pre 1966 file has
   been manually filmed.

GODFREY MEMORIAL LIBRARY
Middletown, CT 06457

Tel: 203/DI-6-4375
Acting Director: Doris Post
Microformats offered: microfiche; micro-opaque cards
Micropublication programs: Genealogical materials on microfiche (older
   materials are on microcards); Annual Corporation Reports, U.S. Federal
   Register and New York Law Journal.

GORDON AND BREACH SCIENCE PUBLISHERS LTD.
41/42 William IV Street, London WC2 England

Tel: 01-836-5125
Telex: 23258
Cable Address: SCIENCEPUB London WC2
Chairman: Martin Gordon (New York)
President: Ena Adam (London)
Controller: Vilma Robinett
Microform Service: Chrisopher Rivington (London)

U.S.A. Office: GORDON AND BREACH SCIENCE PUBLISHERS INC.
1 Park Avenue, New York, NY 10016

Tel: 212/689-0360
Telex: 236735
Cable Address: SCIENCEPUB
Microformats offered: microfiche; 16mm and 35mm microfilm
Micropublication programs: Microform editions of all journals published by
   Gordon and Breach, both current issues and back volumes supplied on
   microfilm or microfiche.

GRAPHIC MICROFILM, INC.
P.O. Box 489, Randolph, MA 02368

Microformats offered: 16mm and 35mm microfilm
Micropublication programs: State Agricultural Experiment Station
publications.

GREAT BRITAIN. PUBLIC RECORD OFFICE
See: Public Record Office

GREENWOOD PRESS
51 Riverside Ave., Westport, CT 06880

Tel: 203/226-3571
Telex: 710-457-3586
Cable Address: Greenpress Westport Connecticut
President: Robert Hagelstein
Controller: Brian Flesher
Marketing Director: D. Farrell Davis
Microformats offered: microfiche (including color); 35mm microfilm
Micropublication programs: Greenwood Press micropublishes periodical
    collections and research collections for libraries as well as the Urban
    Documents Microfiche Collection, documents indexed in the Index to
    Current Urban Documents.

GREGG MUSIC SOURCES
Newton K. Gregg/Publisher, Inc., P.O. Box 1459, Rohnert Park, CA 94928

Tel: 707/526-3161; 707/632-5387
President: Newton K. Gregg
Microformats offered: microfiche
Micropublication programs: Micropublishes unique and rare primary and
    secondary music sources from the ninth through the twentieth centuries.

WALTER DE GRUYTER, INC.
3 Westchester Plaza, Elmsford, NY 10523

Tel: 914/592-5890
General Manager: Eckart A. Scheffler
Microformats offered: 35mm microfilm
Micropublication programs: Complete runs of de Gruyter's journals in the field
   of theology on 35mm microfilm.

HARVARD UNIVERSITY PRESS
79 Garden Street, Cambridge, MA 02138

Tel: 617/495-2600
Telex: 921484
Director: Arthur J. Rosenthal
Editor-in-Chief; Maud Wilcox
Comptroller: Brain P. Murphy
Promotion Manager: Betty Zirnite
Sales Manager: Gary Lawton
Manager, Customer Service: David Tebo
Microformats offered: microfiche
Micropublication programs: Provinces in Rebellion: A Documentary History of
   the Founding of the Commonwealth of Massachusetts, 1774-1775—L.
   Kinvin Wroth, Editor-in-Chief.

HARVESTER PRESS LTD.
2 Stanford Terrace, Hassocks, North Brighton, Sussex, England; Microform
Department, 17 Ship Street, Brighton, Sussex, England

Tel: Brighton 5532 & 4378
Telex: 24224 Mono ref. 2073
Cable Address: Harvester Hassocks
Publisher: John Spiers
Sales Manager: Mark Holland
Customer Services and Accounts: Reg Pickett
Director of Microform Publications: Alastair Everitt
Editor-in-Chief: Robert Baldock
Editors: Dexter Dymoke, Brenda Harris, Molly Colwell, Mavis Thomas
Microformats offered: microfiche; 35mm microfilm
Micropublication programs: Microform collections of source materials of
   British political and social history including a program of Sixteenth and
   Seventeenth Century History. Microfiche edition of Keesing's
   Contemporary Archives, 1931-1975.

WILLIAM S. HEIN & CO., INC. MICRO-FILM DIVISION
1285 Main St., Buffalo, NY 14209

Tel: 716/882-2600
Manager: (Mrs.) Bonnie L. Morton
Microformats offered: microfiche; 16mm and 35mm microfilm
Micropublication programs: Pennsylvania Side Reports; New York Records
    and Briefs; Law Reviews; United States government publications.

HELIOS
Pawlet, VT 05761

Tel: 802/325-3360
President: Tom Burnside
Microformats offered: 35mm microfilm
Micropublication programs: Nineteenth century photographic periodicals.

HER MAJESTY'S STATIONERY OFFICE
Atlantic House, Holborn Viaduct, London EC1P 1BN England

Tel: 01-248-9876
Telex: 22805
Cable Address: Hemstonery, London EC1
Director of Publications Group: D.C. Dashfield
Director of Publishing: B.C.E. Lee
Director of Publications Distribution: J.P. Morgan
Director of Publications Marketing: D. Perry
Microformats offered: microfiche; 35mm microfilm
Micropublication programs: Microfiche Supplement to the London Gazette;
    Third London Commission on Airport; U.K. Continental Shelf, Well Records.

HEYDEN & SON LIMITED
Spectrum House, Alderton Crescent, London NW4 3XX, England

Tel: 01-202-5333
Telex: 28303
Cable Address: Heyspectra London
Managing Director: Gunter Heyden
Publications Director: Peter Williams
Customer Service: Joy Saunders
Microformats offered: 35mm microfilm
Micropublication programs: Biomedical Mass Spectrometry; Journal of
    Thermal Analysis; Organic Magnetic Resonance; Organic Mass
    Spectrometry; X-Ray Spectrometry; Mecke and Langenbucher, Infrared
    Spectra of Selected Organic Compounds.

HIGH DENSITY SYSTEMS
See: University Music Editions

HILL MONASTIC MANUSCRIPT LIBRARY
Bush Center, St. John's University, Collegeville, MN 56321

Tel: 612/363-3514
Director: Dr. Julian G. Plante
Manuscript Catalogers: Fr. Roland Behrendt, O.S.B., Br. Gregory Sebastian,
    Obl. O.S.B., Dr. Donald Yates, Dr. Hope Mayo
Catalogers of Oriental Manuscripts: Dr. William F. Macomber and Dr.
    Getatchew Haile
Microformats offered: 35mm microfilm (including color)
Micropublication programs: Hill Monastic Manuscript Library is a research
    organization which microfilms handwritten records for research purposes.
    They do not sell these films, but publish guides to their collections and invite
    scholars to use their facilities. Copies of Hill's materials can be made only
    with the explicit written permission of the European or African libraries
    owning the original documents. The microform collection is of ancient,
    medieval, Renaissance and early modern manuscripts (*codices
    manuscripti*) of literary/historical type and document archives, with
    emphasis on pre 1600 materials.

HISTORICAL SOCIETY OF PENNSYLVANIA
1300 Locust Street, Philadelphia, PA 19107

Tel: 215/732-6200
Director: James E. Mooney
Chief of Manuscripts: Peter J. Parker
Microformats offered: 35mm microfilm
Micropublication programs: Papers of William Penn; Papers of The
   Pennsylvania Abolition Society; Papers of President James Buchanan;
   Papers of Tench Coxe; various colonial and early national period
   Philadelphia newspapers.

HOOVER INSTITUTION PRESS
Stanford University, Stanford, CA 94305

Tel: 415/321-2300 ext.3373
General manager: Mickey Hamilton
Microform Assistant: Ann Saadus
Microformats offered: 35mm microfilm
Micropublication programs: The Hoover Institution micropublishes its holdings
   of documentation and research on problems of political, social and
   economic change in the twentieth century. The six principal area collections
   are: Africa, East Asia, Eastern Europe and the Soviet Union, Latin America,
   the Middle East and Western Europe.

HUMAN RELATIONS AREA FILE
P.O. Box 2054 Yale Station, 755 Prospect St., New Haven, CT 06520

Tel: 203/777-2334
Director of Educational Programs: Robert O. Lagace
Microformats offered: microfiche
Micropublication programs: Social science source materials representing
   books, articles, and manuscripts selected by experts in cultural and area
   studies. The source materials in each file are organized by subject,
   according to a special subject classification system.

IDAL, INFORMACIÓN DOCUMENTAL DE AMÉRICA LATINA
4824 Ch. Côte des Neiges, Montréal, Qué., Canada H3V 1G4

Tel: 514/735-5945
Director: Alejandro de Corro
Microformats offered: microfiche
Micropublication programs: Dossiers on Microfiche, original documents
   produced in Latin America in Spanish or Portuguese.

ILLINOIS STATE HISTORICAL LIBRARY
Old State Capitol, Springfield, IL 62706

Tel: 217/782-4836
State Historian: William K. Alderfer
Curator of Manuscripts: Paul Spence
Microformats offered: 35mm microfilm
Micropublication programs: Pierre Menard Collection.

IMMIGRATION HISTORY RESEARCH CENTER
University of Minnesota, 826 Berry Street, St. Paul, MN 55114

Tel: 612/373-5581
Director: Rudolph J. Vecoli
Administrative Assistant: Sandra Keith
Microformats offered: microfiche; 35mm microfilm
Micropublication programs: Periodicals of American ethnic and immigrant
   groups from eastern and southern Europe; Polish Microfilm Project;
   Carpatho-Ruthenian Microfilm Project.

INFORMAÇÕES, MICROFORMAS E SISTEMAS S/A (IMS)
Rua Mateus Grou, 57, São Paulo, Brazil

Tel: 280-4759; 853-6680
Publisher: Fredric M. Litto
Microformats offered: 35mm microfilm
Micropublication programs: Brazilian dissertations on microform.

INFORMATION DESIGN INC.
3247 Middlefield Rd., Menlo Park, CA 94025

Tel: 415/369-2962
Chairman of the Board: F. Ward Paine
President: Sam B. Puckett
Vice President, Finance: Steve Halprin
Vice President, Research and Development: Lyle Priest
Microformats offered: Computer-Output-Microfilm
Micropublication programs: Computer-Output-Microfilm card catalogs for
    libraries.

INFORMATION HANDLING SERVICES
15 Inverness Way East, Englewood, CO 80150

Tel: 303/779-0600
Twx: 910/935-0715
President: Edward M. Lee
Senior Vice President: Louis B. Nelson
Editorial Director: Herbert C. Cohen
Senior Market Manager: Stephen J. Mulvihill
Manager, New Product Development: Judith C. Russell
Manager, Hardcopy Publishing: Stefanie Prigge
Library Market Specialist: Edward J. Halloran
Microformats offered: microfiche (including ultramicrofiche); 16mm and 35mm
    microfilm
Micropublication programs: IHS solves information problems for U.S.
    government, industry, and the military; for the legal and medical
    professions, for universities, colleges, and public and law libraries; for U.S.,
    state, county and municipal governments, and for businesses and
    governments throughout the world.

INFORMATION RESOURCES PRESS, A Division of Herner & Co.
2100 M Street, N.W., Suite 316, Washington, DC 20037

Tel: 202/293-2605
Microformats offered: microfiche
Micropublication programs: EIS: Key to Environmental Impact Statements
    makes available the full statements on microfiche.

INGRAM BOOK COMPANY
347 Reedwood Drive, Nashville, TN 37217

Tel: 615/889-3000
President: Harry Hoffman
Microformats offered: microfiche
Micropublication programs: Micro-Bulletin, a library acquistion assistance
   service.

INSPEC (Information Services for the Physics and Engineering Communities)
Savoy Place, London WC2R OBL England

Tel: 01-240-1871
Telex: 261176
Director: D.H. Barlow
Deputy Director: T.M. Aitchison
Microformats offered: 16mm and 35mm microfilm
Micropublication programs: Physics Abstracts, Electrical and Electronic
   Abstracts, Computer and Control Abstracts.

**INSTITUT D'ETHNOLOGIE. MUSÉUM NATIONAL D'HISTOIRE
   NATURELLE** (Collection Archives et Documents)
Musée de l'Homme. Palais de Chaillot, place du Trocadéro 75116 Paris,
   France

Tel: 553-82-15
Directors: Professeur André Leroi-Gourhan and Professeur Jean Guiart
Secretary General: Geneviève Debrégeas-Laurenie
Microformats offered: microfiche
Micropublication programs: Archives et Documents publishes micro-editions
   of new or unpublished texts, theses, genealogical accounts, field-notes,
   documents dealing with rupestre art, ethnology, archeology and pre-history.

THE INSTITUTE FOR ADVANCED STUDIES OF WORLD RELIGIONS
5001 Melville Memorial Library, SUNY-Stony Brook, New York, NY 11794

Tel: 516/246-8362
President: C.T. Shen
Director of Research: C.S. George
Microformats offered: microfiche
Micropublication programs: Demand micropublication with now over 20,000
titles available in microform in the area of world religions.

INSTITUTE OF ELECTRICAL AND ELECTRONICS ENGINEERS (IEEE)
345 E. 47th St., New York, NY 10017

Tel: information, 212/644-7557; orders, 201/981-0060
Director: E.K. Gannett
Managing Editor: W.R. Crone
Microformats offered: microfiche; 16mm and 35mm microfilm
Micropublication programs: All 37 of the IEEE technical journals are available
in microform. Microfiche are issued on a current subscription (issue by
issue) basis. Backfiles of all IEEE periodicals and those of the American
Institute of Electrical Engineers and the Institute of Radio Engineers, are
available on roll microfilm.

THE INSTITUTE OF PAPER CHEMISTRY
1043 East South River Street, Appleton, WI 54911

Tel: 414/734-9251
Director, Division of Information Services: W.S. McClenahan
Editor: Curtis Brown
Microformats offered: microfiche; 16mm microfilm
Micropublication programs: Publishes microfilm and microfiche editions of the
Abstract Bulletin of the Institute of Paper Chemistry.

THE INSTITUTE OF PHYSICS, Publishing Division
Techno House, Redcliffe Way, Bristol BS1 6NX, England

Tel: 0272-297481
Telex: 449149
Director of Publishing: C.I. Pederson
Circulation Manager: I.G. Sadler
Microformats offered: microfiche; 35mm microfilm
Micropublication programs: Microfiche versions of all current volumes of all
   journals and periodicals. Microfilm version for archival material.

INTER DOCUMENTATION COMPANY AG
Postrasse 14, Zug, Switzerland

Tel: 42-214974
Telex: 788 19 ZUGAL
Cable Address: INDOCO Zug
President: Dr. Lelio Vieli
Manager: Herbert Eichenberger
Head Order Dept: Roswitha Heinzer-Fähndrich
IDC's Processing Plant:
INTER DOCUMENTATION COMPANY BV
Uiterstegracht 45, Leiden, The Netherlands

Tel: 071-142700
Cable Address: INTERMICRO
Director: Henri L. de Mink
Microformats offered: microfiche; 35mm microfilm
Micropublication programs: Micropublishers of over 400,000 volumes,
   covering 45 subjects. Selection of titles by specialists at IDC's invitation.
   Itemized catalogues by subject available free on request. Any title or volume
   listed may be ordered separately.

INTERNATIONAL LABOUR OFFICE, PUBLICATIONS (Permanent
Secretariat of the International Labour Organisation, a specialised agency
associated with the United Nations)
CH-1211 Geneva 22, Switzerland

Tel: 99-61-11
Telex: 22-271
Cable Address: INTERLAB, GENEVA
Director General: Francis Blanchard
General Sales Manager (Publications): Ivan M.C.S. Elsmark
Marketing Co-ordinator (Publications): N. Monod
Chief Accountant: A. Cecconi
Customer Service: M. Sulmoni
Rights and Permissions: S. Peters
Microformats offered: microfiche
Micropublication programs: The aim of the ILO micropublishing program is to
make available out-of-print series and periodicals published by the
Organisation in the social and labour fields.

INTERNATIONAL MICROFORM DISTRIBUTION SERVICE (IMDS), A
Division of Clearwater Publishing Company, Inc.
1995 Broadway, Room 401, New York, NY 10023

Tel: 212/873-2100
President: Norman A. Ross
Customer Service: Maureen Grice
Canadian Office: 231 Hollyberry Trail, Willowdale, Ontario, Canada M2H 2 P3

Tel: 416/494-6143
Director Dr. Lewis J. Rosen
Microformats offered: microfiche; 16mm and 35mm microfilm
Micropublication programs: IMDS offers U.S. and Canadian libraries a single
source for all foreign microforms, regardless of country and publisher. All
publications are sold at list price—or less—payable in either U.S. or
Canadian dollars. Regular IMDS clients are provided with a 5% discount on
all purchases where such discounts are permitted to IMDS by the foreign
publisher.

INTERNATIONAL TRADE CENTRE
Palais des Nations, CH-1211, Genève 10, Switzerland

Tel: 31-12-55
Telex: 28 90 52
Cable Address: Intradcen, Geneva
Chief, Market Intelligence Service: Istvan Agoston
Microformats offered: microfiche
Micropublication programs: Import Tabulation System.

IRISH MICROFORMS LTD.
124 Ranelagh, Dublin 6, Ireland

Tel: (01) 961133
Director: S.I. Browne
Microformats offered: microfiche; 35mm microfilm
Micropublication programs: British Diplomatic Blue Books, Anglo-Irish
    literature, Northern Ireland political literature, Irish political and radical
    newspapers of the twentieth century and Irish studies.

JEWISH CHRONICLE LIMITED, A Part of Jewish Chronicle Newspapers
    Limited
25 Furnival Street, London, EC4A 1JT, England

Tel: 01-405 9252
Telex: 28452
Sales Manager: M. Weinberg
Microformats offered: 16mm and 35mm microfilm
Micropublication programs: The Jewish Chronicle 1841-1976 on 35mm
    microfilm and The Jewish Chronicle Index 1841-1895 on 16mm microfilm.

JOHNSON ASSOCIATES INC.
P.O. Box 1017, 321 Greenwich Ave., Greenwich, CT 06830

Tel: 203/661-7602
President: Herbert M. Johnson
Operations & Customer Service Mgr.: Linda Sidor
Manager, Publisher Relations: Mrs. Vel Engels
Manager, Accounting Department: Joan Armstrong
Microformats offered: microfiche
Micropublication programs: Scholarly periodicals and research collections in microfiche. McCarthy Memorial Collection of Alcohol Literature. JSAS: Catalog of Selected Documents in Psychology. Reform of Local Government Structures in the U.S. 1945-1971.

JUTA & COMPANY LIMITED
Mercury Crescent, Welton 7790; P.O. Box 123, Kenwyn 7790, South Africa

Tel: 71-1181
Managing Director: J. Douglas Duncan
Microformats offered: microfiche
Micropublication programs: South African Law Reports 1828-1946.

KTO MICROFORM DIVISION
Route 100, Millwood, NY 10546

Tel: 914/762-2200
Telex: 710/573-2328
Cable Address: KTOL Millwood New York
President: Herbert W. Gstalder
Manager: Richard J. McGowan
Customer Service: Anthony M. Mitura
Microformats offered: microfiche; 16mm and 35mm microfilm
Micropublication programs: KTO offers serials in a variety of subject areas. Special programs include Public Records of Great Britain, Boston Symphony Orchestra Program Notes, Early American Children's Books, Titles from the Schomburg Center for Research in Black Culture and State Censuses.

LAW REPRINTS, INC.
37 West 20th Street, New York, NY 10011

Tel: 212/242-5358
Projects Manager: Lincoln Fisher
Microformats offered: microfiche
Micropublication programs: Law Reprints micropublishes the records and
briefs of all cases handled by the U.S. Supreme Court and various other
major courts.

LAWRENCE NEWSPAPERS, INC., Lawrence Microfilming Service
P.O. Box 1015, Fuquay-Varina, NC 27526

Tel: 919/552-5178
President: Lewis H. Lawrence
Microformats offered: microfiche; 16mm and 35mm microfilm; micro-opaque
cards
Micropublication programs: Microfilming of engineering drawings,
newspapers and source documents.

H.R. LAWRENCE PUBLICATIONS
308 Sackett Building, University Park, PA 16802

Tel: 814/865-9535
Microformats offered: microfiche
Micropublication programs: Visual Communication Products and other
materials for students of architecture.

LEEDS POLYTECHNIC SCHOOL OF LIBRARIANSHIP
28 Park Place, Leeds LS1 2SY, United Kingdom

Tel: 0532-456696
Microformats offered: microfiche
Micropublication programs: The Research Report Series has one title
available on microfiche—The Usage of Periodicals in Public Libraries.

LIBRARY MICROFILMS, A Division of Bay Microfilm Inc.
737 Loma Verde Ave., Palo Alto, CA 94303

Tel: 415/494-1812
President: Wm. D. Whitney
Vice President: Thos. D. Whitney
Secretary/Treasurer: Dorothy Chrisman
Library Specialist: Joan Gatenby
Microformats offered: microfiche; 16mm and 35mm microfilm
Micropublication programs: Over 300 newspaper titles particularly in
    California, Nevada and Pacific Northwest. Early California history on roll film
    and microfiche.

THE LIBRARY OF CONGRESS, PHOTODUPLICATION SERVICE
10 First Street,S.E., Washington, DC 20540

Tel: 202/426-5652
Telex: 710-822-0185
Chief: Charles G. LaHood, Jr.
Assistant Chief for Bibliographic Services: Carolyn Hoover Sung
Assistant Chief for Technical Services: Elmer S. King
Head, Public Services Section: William E. Younger
Microformats offered: microfiche; 16mm and 35mm microfilm
Micropublication programs: The Library of Congress Photoduplication Service
    provides microform reproductions of research materials which are filmed as
    part of the Library's microfilm preservation program. Most of the resource
    material available through this service is unique or scarce.

LIBRARY RESOURCES INC.
425 N. Michigan Ave., Chicago, IL 60611

Tel: 312/321-7444
President: Herman C. Bernick
Microformats offered: ultramicrofiche
Micropublication programs: Microbook Library of American Civilization;
    Microbook Library of English Literature.

LOMOND PUBLICATIONS
P.O. Box 56, Mt. Airy, MD 21771

Tel: 301/829-1633
President: Lowell H. Hattery
Microformats offered: microfiche
Micropublication programs: Microfiche editions of books on management,
   science policy and technological change.

LOST CAUSE PRESS
750-56 Starks Bldg., Louisville, KY 40202

Tel: 502/584-8404
Cable Address: Lostcaus Louisville
Consultant: Charles Farnsley
President: Nancy Farnsley
Vice-President:Alex Farnsley
Vice-President: Burrel Farnsley
Microformats offered: microfiche
Micropublication programs: Micropublication of nineteenth century American
   literature and history and various British and European scholarly works not
   readily available in book form.

THE FREDERIC LUTHER COMPANY
2803 East 56th Street, Indianapolis, IN 46220

Tel: 317/253-3446
Partner: Frederic Luther
Microformats offered: microfiche; 35mm microfilm
Micropublication programs: Specializes in micropublication of historical,
   genealogical and scientific publications.

MCLAREN MICROPUBLISHING
P.O. Box 972, Station F, Toronto, Canada M4Y 2N9

Tel: 416/461-1627
Proprietor: Duncan McLaren
Microformats offered: microfiche; 16mm and 35mm microfilm
Micropublication programs: Mainly primary sources in Canadian social and
   political history, with an emphasis on retrospective newspapers and serials.

MACLEAN-HUNTER LIMITED MICROFILM SERVICES
481 University Ave., Toronto, Ont., Canada M5W 1A7

Tel: 416/595-1811
Manager, Microfilm Services: Nigel Golding
Media Coordinator: Merrilyn Menzies
Microformats offered: microfiche; 35mm microfilm
Micropublication programs: Canadian newspapers and periodicals on
microfilm or microfiche and a comprehensive list of vertical file topics on a
monthly basis.

MANCHESTER PUBLIC LIBRARIES
Central Library, St. Peter's Square, Manchester 2 England

Microformats offered: 35mm microfilm
Micropublication programs: Manchester Evening News; Manchester
Guardian 1821-1952; 25 Reels U.S. Tracts 18 & 19th Centuries; Stockport
Advertiser: Athletic News; Salford Newspapers; Party Registers and
Directories.

MANSELL INFORMATION/PUBLISHING LTD.
3 Bloomsbury Place, London, WC1A 2QA England

Tel: 01-580-6784
Cable Address: Infoman London
Chairman: John E. Commander
Managing Director: John E. Duncan
Editorial Manager: David Powell
Sales Manager: June S. Eaton
Promotion Manager: Catherine Johnston
Production Manager: Faith Cheesman
Microformats offered: microfiche; 16mm and 35mm microfilm
Micropublication programs: Microform is only one of the media of publication
used by Mansell, who do publish their four periodicals in microfiche as well
as paper and who often do keep books in print by 'reprinting' in microfiche.
Mansell, therefore, has no micropublishing programme as such, but elects
to publish a title in microform when that medium is most suitable or when the
market is so small that microform is the only way a title can be published
viably.

MARC APPLIED RESEARCH COMPANY, A Division of the Library Corporation
P.O. Box 40035, Washington, DC 20016

Tel: 301/840-1480
Product Manager: Brower Murphy
Microformats offered: microfiche
Micropublication programs: MARCFICHE: Library of Congress and contributed cataloguing with five cumulative indexes, updated weekly.

MARYLAND HISTORICAL SOCIETY
201 W. Monument St., Baltimore, MD 20201

Tel: 301/685-3750
Director: P. William Filby
Assistant Director and Curator: Romaine Somerville
Curator of Manuscripts: Richard Cox
Microformats offered: 16mm and 35mm microfilm
Micropublication programs: Lloyd Family Papers; Papers of the Maryland Colonization Society; John Pendleton Kennedy Papers; William Wirt Papers; Calvert Family Papers; Mordicai Gist Papers; Charles Carroll of Carrollton Papers; David Baillie Warden Papers; Robert Goodloe Harper Papers; Minutes of the Trustees of the Poor for Baltimore City and County; Benjamin Henry Latrobe Papers.

MASSACHUSETTS HISTORICAL SOCIETY
1154 Boylston St., Boston, MA 02215

Tel: 617/536-1608
Microformats offered: 35mm microfilm
Micropublication programs: Production of microfilm editions (some with Guides) of significant, rare, or heavily used original materials in the collections of the Massachusetts Historical Society. Microfilm publications include The Adams Papers; Papers of Cotton Mather; Quincy, Wendell, Holmes, and Upham Family papers; Winthrop Papers.

MEIKLEJOHN CIVIL LIBERTIES INSTITUTE
1715 Francisco St., Berkeley, CA 94703

Tel: 415/848-0599
President: Ann Fagan Ginger
Librarian: Ann Lawson
Librarian: David Christiano
Microformats offered: 35mm microfilm
Micropublication programs: The Angela Davis Trial; The Pentagon Papers
Trial, California V Savio, et. al.; Civil Liberties Publications; Harry Bridges
1938-52.

THE MICHIE COMPANY
P.O. Box 57, Charlottesville, VA 22902

Tel: 804/295-6171
President: D.W. Parrish
Vice President and Secretary: S.G. Alrich
Executive Assistant to President: M. Paul Cook
Sales Manager: J.G. Gilbert
Microformats offered: micro-opaque cards
Micropublication programs: Virginia Supreme Court of Appeals reports 1-212.

MICRO-COMFAX INC.
925 Kranzel Drive, Camp Hill, PA 17011

Tel: 717/761-5030
Microformats offered: 35mm microfilm
Micropublication programs: Pennsylvania newspapers.

MICRODOC
815 Carpenter Lane, Philadelphia, PA 19119

Tel: 215/848-4545
Proprietor: Thomas F. Deahl
Microformats offered: microfiche
Micropublication programs: Original mongraphs.

MICROÉDITIONS HACHETTE
6, rue Casimir Delavigne-75006 Paris, France

Tel: 329-77-41
Head of Department: Jean-Pierre Michaud
Editor: Léon Centner
Microformats offered: microfiche
Micropublication programs: Micropublisher of rare, old, significant French
   thematic collections of historical research works, particularly political,
   economics, social history, all presented by renowned academics.

MICROÉDITIONS UNIVERSITAIRES
See: Fondation Nationale des Sciences Politiques

MICROFICHE FOUNDATION
101 Doelenstraat Delft The Netherlands

Tel: 015-133222-ext.5677
Telex: 31448 (Library Technological University Delft IFLA-telecode)
President: Dr. J. Zandvliet
Editor MF Newsletter: Ms. A. de Bruin
Microformats offered: microfiche
Micropublication programs: The Microfiche Foundation is an international,
   non-commercial organization devoted to the propagation of the use of
   microfiche. The Foundation publishes a Newsletter three to four times
   annually, and issues booklets on microfiche matters in its series
   Publications on the Microfiche.

MICROFICHE PUBLICATIONS, a Division of Microfiche Systems
  Corporation
440 Park Ave. So., New York, NY 10016

Tel: 212/679-3132
President: Cy Brownstein
Marketing Director: G. Maltese
Microformats offered: microfiche
Micropublication programs: A registered agent for all NTIS enviro/energy
  materials; producer of Envirofiche; international reports; Language and
  Linguistics MicroLibrary collection; Public Papers of Presidents: Truman,
  Eisenhower, Kennedy and Johnson.

MICROFILE LIMITED
P.O. Box 61328, Marshalltown, 2107, Johannesburg, South Africa

Tel: 836-7662
Telex: 8-6998 SA
Chairman: D.H. Farrant
Manager: D.F. Collins
Microformats offered: 35mm microfilm
Micropublication programs: South African newspapers.

MICROFILM ASSOCIATION OF GREAT BRITAIN
1 and 2 Trinity Churchyard, High St. Guildford, Surrey, England

Tel: Godalming 6653
Director General: G.G. Baker
Editor: S.J. Teague
Microformats offered: microfiche
Micropublication programs: Fiche copies of published edition of the quarterly
  journal of the Association—"Microdoc."

MICROFILM CENTER, INC.
P.O. Box 45436, Dallas, TX 75235

Tel: 214/358-5231
President: Harvey G. Rust
Vice President: D.L. Rhea
Secretary/Treasurer: Patricia Rust
Sales: Bob White, Dave Sawyer
Microformats offered: microfiche; 16mm and 35mm microfilm
Micropublication programs: Periodicals, out-of-print books, Church Records,
   and newspapers.

MICROFILM CORPORATION OF PENNSYLVANIA
141 South Highland Ave., Pittsburgh, PA 15206

Tel: 412/661-9280
Microformats offered: microfiche; 16mm and 35mm microfilm
Micropublication programs: Primarily a service microfilm company. Projects
   include filming newspapers dating from 1200 to present and engineering
   drawings (filmed according to customer requirements).

MICROFILMING CORPORATION OF AMERICA
21 Harristown Rd., Glen Rock, NJ 07452

Tel: 201/447-3000
President: Karl Horwitz
Vice President, Operations: Robert C. Olson
Vice President, Editorial: Edward A. Reno
Vice President, Research and Development: Don M. Avedon
Director of Marketing: Donald J. Ellis
Microformats offered: microfiche; 35mm microfilm
Micropublication programs: Major micropublisher of newspapers (including
   The New York Times, Financial Times, Atlanta Constitution); periodicals
   (including Viewpoint: America's Syndicated Journalists on File) and special
   collections.

MICROFORM REVIEW, INC.
520 Riverside Ave., P.O. Box 405 Saugatuck Station, Westport, CT 06880

Tel: 203/226-6967
Publisher: Alan Marshall Meckler
Editor-in-Chief: Allen B. Veaner
Editor-in-Chief, Book Division: John J. Walsh
Managing Editor: Jeanne Short
Microformats offered: microfiche; 35mm microfilm
Micropublication programs: Micropublishers' Trade List Annual; International File of Micrographics Equipment & Accessories; Microform Review on microfiche.

MICROFORMS INTERNATIONAL MARKETING CORPORATION,
A Subsidiary of Pergamon Press, Inc.
Fairview Park, Elmsford, NY 10523

Tel: 914/592-9143
Telexes: 13:7328
Cable Address: Pergapress Emfd
President: Dr. Edward Gray
Marketing: Sotir Nikola
Sales: I. Benz
Production: I. Benglas
Accounting: Sheldon J. Aboff
Microformats offered: microfiche; 16mm and 35mm microfilm
Micropublication programs: Micropublishing and microdistributor of scholarly serials and collections. Exclusive micropublishers of Pergamon Press publications. Simultaneous micropublications of journals and U.S. government serials. Licensed micropublisher of HMSO Parliamentary Debates.

MICROGRAPHIC PUBLICATION SERVICE
5455 Wilshire Blvd., Suite 1009, Los Angeles, CA 90036

Tel: 213/938-5274
Managing Editor: Carol A. Platt
Microformats offered: microfiche (including color)
Micropublication programs: Micropublishers whose primary interests are in the re-publication of scholarly reference works and in the publication of photographic archives on microfiche.

MICROGRAPHICS AUSTRALASIA
Box 414, P.O. Artarmon, N.S.W. Australia 2064

Microformats offered: microfiche
Micropublication programs: Micropublication of the monthly magazine "Micrographics Australasia" produced for members of the Microfilm Association of Australia Ltd.

MICROGRAPHICS II
Rt. 7, Box 258G, Charlottesville, VA 22901

Tel: 804/296-0596
President: Don W. Massey
Customer Service: Mrs. Susan B. Gray
Microformats offered: 35mm microfilm
Micropublication programs: Americana on microfilm; Eighteenth-Century English Literature and Culture.

MICROINFO LTD.
P.O. Box 3, Alton, Hampshire, GU 34 1EF England

Tel: Alton 84300
Telex: 858431
Editorial Director: Roy Selwyn
Microformats offered: microfiche; 16mm microfilm
Micropublication programs: Back volumes of Microinfo's own newsletters and the full range of reports and periodicals offered by the National Technical Information Service of the U.S. Department of Commerce.

MICROLOGUE, INC.
2010 Curtis St., Denver, CO 80205

Tel: 303/892-9344
President: Rick Puttmann
Microformats offered: microfiche
Micropublication programs: College and University Catalogs on Microfiche.

MICROMEDIA LIMITED
Box 502, Station S, Toronto, Canada M5M 4L8

Tel: 416/489-8016
President: Robert Gibson
Microformats offered: microfiche; 16mm and 35mm microfilm
Micropublication programs: Canadian federal, provincial, and urban documents; Canadian Parliamentary Papers; Canadian journals and newspapers.

MICROPUBLISHING INTERNATIONAL LTD.
82 Edgely Lane, Clapham, London SW4, England

Microformats offered: microfiche; 16mm and 35mm microfilm
Micropublication programs: A range of journals, including those published by Gordon & Breach and Pergamon.

MICROTEXT LIBRARY SERVICES
See: James T. White Co.

MICRO-URBA, French Information System for Urban and Regional Planning
BP 241 13605 Aix en Provence, France

Tel: (42) 27-68-37
Manager: Dominique Gille
Microformats offered: microfiche
Micropublication programs: Literature (Government reports, dissertations, surveys) about regional and urban planning in France: Ecology, Leisure, Urban problems, Employment, Demography, Regional policy, Local authorities, Transportation, Urban sociology, Land planning, Regional economics.

MIKROFILMARCHIV DER DEUTSCHSPRACHIGEN PRESSE E.V.
D. 4600 Dortmund, Hansaplatz (Institut für Zeitungsforschung) West
Germany

Tel: 542-23216
Telex: 822287 (Stadt Dortmund)
President: Dr. Roland Seeburg-Elverfeldt
General Secretary: Prof. Dr. Kurt Koszyk
Microformats offered: 35mm microfilm
Micropublication programs: German newspapers and periodicals of
nineteenth and twentieth centuries, especially 1848-49; German exile 1933-
45; labour movement; current periodicals.

MIKROPRESS GMBH
D-53 Bonn, Baunscheidtstr. 17 West Germany

Tel: 231688
Manager: Wilhelm Peters
Microformats offered: microfiche; 35mm microfilm
Micropublication programs: Socialist Movement 1840-1933; Anti-National
Socialist German Exile Press 1933-1945; German Republic 1918-1933;
Press of National Socialism 1920-1945; Newspapers current subscription.

MINDATA LTD.
32 The Mall, London W5 3TW England

Tel: 01-579-1679
Microformats offered: microfiche
Micropublication programs: A Photographic Record of the Principal items in
the collection of The Victoria & Albert Museum.

MINERVA MIKROFILM A/S
2900 Hellerup, Ehlersvej 27, HE 8333 Denmark

Microformats offered: 35mm microfilm
Micropublication programs: Danish newspapers.

MINNESOTA HISTORICAL SOCIETY
Division of Archives and Manuscripts, 1500 Mississippi Street, St. Paul MN
55101

Tel: 612/296-6980
State Archivist: Lucile M. Kane
Deputy State Archivist: Sue E. Holbert
Head of Technical Services: Lydia A. Lucas
Microformats offered: 16mm and 35mm microfilm
Micropublication programs: Archives and manuscripts.

MARY NASH INFORMATION SERVICES
188 Dagmar Ave., Vanier, Ontario, K1L 5T2 Canada

Tel: 613/745-5112
Proprietor: Mary M. Nash
Microformats offered: microfiche
Micropublication programs: Micropublisher of original materials, not
previously published in any form, in any marketable subject. Specialties are
bibliographies and conference proceedings.

NATIONAL DESIGN CENTER, INC.
Instant Data Access Control, 425 E. 53rd Street, New York, NY 10022

Tel: 212/MU-8-5200
President: Norman Ginsberg
Sales: Robert Davis
Microformats offered: microfiche
Micropublication programs: Emphasis on architecture, housing and urban
development. Micropublisher of the Thomas Register of American
Manufacturers.

NATIONAL HISTORICAL PUBLICATION AND RECORDS COMMISSION
National Archives Bldg., Washington, DC 20408

Tel: 202/523-3234
Executive Director: Frank G. Burke
Deputy Executive Director: Fred Shelley
Microformats offered: 35mm microfilm
Micropublication programs: A cooperative program with U.S. archives and
  manuscript repositories to publish on microfilm the papers and records of
  Americans and American organizations that have been significant parts of
  our national history.

NATIONAL INFORMATION CENTER FOR EDUCATIONAL MEDIA
See: NICEM

NATIONAL LIBRARY OF AUSTRALIA
Canberra ACT 2600, Australia

Tel: (062) 621-111
Telex: 62100
Cable Address: Natlibaust Canberra
Principal Librarian: Marie Sexton
Microformats offered: microfiche; 16mm microfilm
Micropublication programs: Microform is used to publish m/r files on COM;
  large card catalogues for wide distribution; research reports or other
  documentation either prepared by the Library or other institutions.

NATIONAL LIBRARY OF CANADA
Canadian Theses Division, Cataloguing Branch, National Library of Canada,
  395 Wellington St., Ottawa, Canada, K1A ON4

Tel: 613/995-9481
Chief of Division: Roy H. Engfield
Microformats offered: microfiche; 35mm microfilm
Micropublication programs: The Division receives original theses, both
  masters' and doctors', from more than 30 Canadian universities. The theses
  are photographed on microfiche and catalogued for the national
  bibliography, *Canadiana*. Copies of the fiches are available for sale to the
  public.

NATIONAL LIBRARY OF SCOTLAND
George IV Bridge, Edinburgh EH1 1EW, Scotland

Tel: 031-226-4531
Telex: 72638 natlibscot edin
Microfilm Information: M. A. Begg
Microformats offered: 35mm microfilm
Micropublication programs: Scottish newspapers; books; collected papers.

NATIONAL MICROFILM LIBRARY
8090 Engineer Road, San Diego, CA 92111

Tel: 714/560-8051 or 1-800/854-2670
President: Harry Cooper
Director of Marketing: Ron Hootman
Microformats offered: microfiche
Micropublication programs: The Microfiche College Catalog Collection is the
    most comprehensive collection of college catalogs ever assembled! More
    than 2,900 colleges and universities represented by 3,700 catalogs.

NATIONAL MICROGRAPHICS ASSOCIATION
8728 Colesville Rd., Silver Spring, MD 20910

Tel: 301/587-8444
Microformats offered: microfiche (including color)
Micropublication programs: Journal of Micrographics; NMA Conference
    Proceedings; reprints from Resource Center collection; Special Interest
    Package series; and Personal Learning Packages on microfiche.

NATIONAL REPROGRAPHIC CENTRE FOR DOCUMENTATION
The Hatfield Polytechnic, Endymion Road Annexe, Hatfield, Herts AL10 8AM
    England
Tel: Hatfield 66144
Director: Bernard J. S. Williams
Head of Research: Alan Horder
Investigator (Evaluation): Roger Broadhurst
Publications Information Officer: John Spencer
Microformats offered: microfiche
Micropublication programs: Simultaneous micropublication with all NRCd
    printed publications, including Research Reports, Equipment Evaluation
    and Systems Case Studies.

NATIONAL TECHNICAL INFORMATION SERVICE (NTIS)
5285 Port Royal Road, Springfield, VA 22161

Tel: 703/557-4630
Subscription Department: Carolyn Starbird
Product Manager: A.W. Alexander 703/557-4734
Microformats offered: microfiche; 16mm and 35mm microfilm
Micropublication programs: Micropublishes U.S. Government reports in
   science and technology and results of government sponsored research.

NEW HAMPSHIRE HISTORICAL SOCIETY
Thirty Park Street, Concord, NH 03301

Tel: 603/226-3381
Editor: Frank C. Mevers
Microformats offered: 35mm microfilm
Micropublication programs: The Papers of Josiah Bartlett.

NEW MEXICO STATE RECORDS CENTER AND ARCHIVES
404 Montezuma, Santa Fe, NM 87501

Tel: 505/827-2321
Chief, Historical Services Division: Dr. Myra Ellen Jenkins
Microformats offered: 35mm microfilm
Micropublication programs: Spanish Archives of New Mexico; Mexican
   Archives of New Mexico; Territorial Archives of New Mexico.

NEW SCIENCE PUBLICATIONS
128 Long Acre, London WC2, England

Microformats offered: microfiche
Micropublication programs: New Science and New Society.

NEW UNIVERSITY PRESS, INC.
520 N. Michigan Ave., Chicago, IL 60611

Tel: 312/828-0420
Editor: Stephen O'Neil
Consultant Editor: Thomas Ferguson
Associate Editor: Victor LaMotte
Microformats offered: microfiche
Micropublication programs: Out-of-print books on microfiche.

NEW YORK LAW JOURNAL
258 Broadway, New York, NY 10007

Tel: 212/964-9400
Microformats offered: 35mm microfilm
Micropublication programs: New York Law Journal, the official daily law paper
 for the first and second judicial departments.

THE NEW YORK MICROFORM JOURNAL FOR MEDICAL ARCHIVES
44 East 67th Street, New York, NY 10021

Editor: Paul S. Striker, M.D.
Microformats offered: 35mm microfilm
Micropublication programs: Archives of New York Medicine.

NEW YORK PUBLIC LIBRARY
Photographic Service, Fifth Avenue & 42nd Street, New York, NY 10018

Tel: 212/790-6262
Microformats offered: 35mm microfilm
Micropublication programs: Preservation microfilming of the library's
 collection, including periodicals and newspapers (domestic and foreign).

THE NEW YORK TIMES INFORMATION BANK
229 West 43rd St., New York, NY 10036

Tel: 212/556-1111
Director: Carl Keil
Microformats offered: microfiche
Micropublication programs: New York Times Information Bank Service.

NEWSBANK, INC.
P.O. Box 10047; 741 Main Street, Stamford, CT 06904

Tel: 203/357-8894
President: Daniel S. Jones
Microformats offered: microfiche
Micropublication programs: NewsBank Library is a current awareness
   reference service in the field of urban and public affairs divided into 13 major
   subject catagories.

NEWSPAPER ARCHIVE DEVELOPMENTS LIMITED
16 Westcote Road, Reading, RG3 2DF, England

Tel: 0734-583247
U.S. Office, P.O. Box 4013, Amity Station, New Haven, CT 06525, U.S.A.
Managing Director: Colin Kyte
Marketing Manager: David Robson
Customer Services Manager: Lorna Payne
Office Manager: Una Callum
Micropublication programs: Micropublishes The Times (London) and other
   serial publications published by the parent company; Times Newspapers
   Limited (marketed outside North America); Le Monde, The Daily Telegraph,
   The Scotsman (marketed worldwide).

NICEM (National Information Center for Educational Media)
University of Southern California, University Park, Los Angeles, CA 90007

Director: M. Thomas Risner
Associate Director: Margaret Vander Schaaf
Microformats offered: microfiche
Micropublication programs: The NICEM indexes of non-print educational
   media are available on microfiche. The indexes are prepared utilizing the
   world's largest data base on non-print educational media.

NORTHERN MICROGRAPHICS
P.O. Box 1653, LaCrosse, WI 54601

Tel: 608/782-4180
President: Frank Jambois
Microformats offered: microfiche; 16mm and 35mm microfilm
Micropublication programs: A microprinter serving both the commercial and
  scholarly marketplace.

JEFFREY NORTON PUBLISHERS, INC.
145 East 49th Street, New York, NY 10017

Tel: 212/753-1783
Marketing: Bruce Salender
Microformats offered: microfiche
Micropublication programs: "Micropapers Editions" is a publication format
  which combines printed abstracts of professional papers with microfiche of
  the corresponding full text packaged together in a conventional hardbound
  book format.

OHIO HISTORICAL SOCIETY
Interstate 71 & 17th Avenue, Columbus, OH 43211

Tel: 614/466-2060
Head Librarian: Anita P. Lunn
Microfilm Specialist: Robert B. Jones
Microformats offered: 16mm and 35mm microfilm
Micropublication programs: 35mm microfilming of Newspapers and
  Manuscript Collections to preserve Ohio History. Stringent quality control
  assures legibility and completeness. Selected contract microfilming is
  encouraged.

GEORG OLMS VERLAG GMBH
Hagentorwall 6-7, D-3200 Hildesheim, West Germany

Tel: (0 51 21) 3-70-07
Publisher: W. Georg Olms
Publishing Manager: Dr. E. Mertens
Publicity Manager: J. Koeltzsch
Microformats offered: microfiche
Micropublication programs: Bibliothek der Deutschen Sprache (a library of
    German literature).

OLYMPIC MEDIA INFORMATION
71 West 23rd Street, New York, NY 10010

Tel: 212/675-4500
Publisher: Walter J. Carroll
Microformats offered: microfiche
Micropublication programs: Micropublisher of audiovisual reference
    directories including: Educational Media Catalogs on Microfiche, Guides to
    Audiovisual Media, Training Film Profiles, Hospital/Health Care Training
    Media Profiles.

OMNIWEST CORPORATION
3322 So. 3rd East, Salt Lake City, UT 84115

Tel: 801/486-3563
Microformats offered: 35mm microfilm
Micropublication programs: Western newspapers and publications of Mormon
    interest.

OXFORD MICROFORM PUBLICATIONS LTD., a member of the Blackwell Group
Blue Boar Street, Oxford OX1 4EY, England

Tel: Oxford 723731
Telex: 83118
Cable Address: Books Oxford
Chairman: Robert Campbell
Managing Director: Peter Ashby
General Manager: Brian Windscheffel
Customer Service: Anne Sheldon
Microformats offered: microfiche (including color); 35mm microfilm
Micropublication programs: Oxford Microform publishes and supplies a wide range of research collections, periodicals and original documents.

OXFORD PUBLISHING COMPANY
5 Lewis Close, Risington, Headington, Oxford, England

Tel: (0865) 66215
Director: Colin Judge
Microformats offered: microfiche
Micropublication programs: Rare books on railways.

OXFORD UNIVERSITY PRESS
200 Madison Ave., New York, NY 10016

Tel: 212/679-7300
Vice-President: Gerald Sussman
Microformats offered: microfiche
Micropublication programs: A special reissue of scholar-selected titles from the Oxford University Press out-of-print list is offered on microfiche. The first series of Oxford University Press Microfiche Editions includes 59 titles in history and 48 in English literature.

PARIS PUBLICATIONS INC.
2 Haven Ave., Port Washington, NY 11050

Tel: 516/883-4650
President: Serge Ciregna
Microformats offered: ultramicrofiche
Micropublication programs: French Books in Print.

PASCOE (W&F) PTY LIMITED
2a Glen St., Milson's Point, N.S.W., 2061 Australia

Microformats offered: 35mm microfilm
Micropublication programs: Australian newspapers and periodicals.

PERCEPTUAL AND MOTOR SKILLS/PSYCHOLOGICAL REPORTS
Box 9229, Missoula, MT 59807

Tel: 406/243-5091
Editors and Publishers: Bruce Ammons and Carol H. Ammons
Microform Publication: Kathy Schwanke
Microformats offered: micro-opaque cards; 16mm microfilm
Micropublication programs: Micropublisher of Perceptual and Motor Skills and
   Psychological Reports. Complete back set available in microform. Each
   publication is microfilmed at the end of subscription year.

PERGAMON PRESS INC.
See: Microforms International Marketing Corp.

PICK PUBLISHING CORPORATION
21 West Street, New York, NY 10006

Tel: 212/944-5960
Cable Address: PICKREPORT
President: Dr. Franz Pick
Controller: Philip Cowitt
Editor: George T. Steve
Promotion Manager: Robin Berger
Customer Service: Helen Emmert
Microformats offered: microfiche; 16mm microfilm
Micropublication programs: All the Monies of the World—A Chronology of
   Currency Values; Common Stocks vs. Gold 1930-1962; Pick's Currency
   Yearbooks 1955-1974 (19 volumes); The United States Dollar—Deflate or
   Devalue.

PLENUM PUBLISHING CORPORATION
227 West 17th Street, New York, NY 10011

Tel: 212/255-0713
Microformats offered: 35mm microfilm
Micropublication programs: Translations of Russian-Soviet journals.

POLLUTION ABSTRACTS/OCEANIC ABSTRACTS
See: Data Courier

H. PORDES
529B, Finchley Rd., London, NW3 7BH England

Tel: 01-435-9879
General Manager: W. H. Gardner
Microformats offered: 35mm microfilm
Micropublication programs: Micropublishers of Palmer's Index to The Times
  Newspaper 1790-1941 (June) on 21 reels of 35mm microfilm.

PRECEDENT PUBLISHING, INC.
520 North Michigan Avenue, Chicago, IL 60611

Tel: 312/828-0420
Microformats offered: microfiche
Micropublication programs: Microfiche reproduction of Gesammelte Schriften
  von Karl Marx und Friedrich Engels.

PREDICASTS, INC.
11001 Cedar Ave., Cleveland, OH 44106

Tel: 216/795-3000
Director, Microform Services: Barbara J. Peck
Microformats offered: microfiche
Micropublication programs: Predicasts, a basic tool for long range planning.

PRESBYTERIAN HISTORICAL SOCIETY
425 Lombard St., Philadelphia, PA 19147

Tel: 215/MA-7-1852
Microformats offered: 35mm microfilm
Micropublication programs: Historical books and documents of importance in
the historical development of Presbyterianism.

THE PRETORIA STATE LIBRARY
P.O. Box 397, Pretoria, South Africa

Tel: 48-3920
Telex: 3-778 SA
Director: Dr. H. J. Aschenborn
Microformats offered: microfiche; 35mm microfilm
Micropublication programs: The Natal Witness (1884-1901), The
Potchefstroom Herald and Wester Gazette (1909-1977), The Bloemfontein
Post (1901-1915), Republic of South Africa Government Gazette (1910-
1972), Western Transvaal Record (1969-1977).

PRINCETON DATAFILM, INC.
P.O. Box 231, Princeton Jct. NJ 08550

Tel: 609/799-1630
Chairman: Theodore C. Slosson, Jr.
President: Claude R. Frazer
Microformats offered: microfiche; 16mm and 35mm microfilm
Micropublication programs: German Judaica—Serial Periodicals (foreign
language) of German Jewish Community from mid 1800s to its end with the
rise to power of Hitler (late 1930s).Synergetics Dictionary—Concepts,
definitions and generalized principles discovered or formulated by
Buckminster Fuller.

PRINCETON MICROFILM CORPORATION
Alexander Road, Princeton, NJ 08540

Tel: 609/452-2066
President: Franklin D. Crawford
Vice President of Sales and Marketing: Anthony DeStephen
Vice President of Advertising: Clifford Crawford
Executive Sales Director: Corrie Van Der Lee
Production Manager: Carl Weir
Microformats offered: 16mm and 35mm microfilm
Micropublication programs: Micropublishers of serials in all subject areas and
    NTIS Reference File.

PUBLIC RECORD OFFICE
Ruskin Avenue, Kew, Richmond, Surrey TW9 4DU, England

Tel: 01-876-3444
Chancery Lane, London WC2 1LR, England

Tel: 01-405-0741
Keeper of Public Records: J. R. Ede
Microformats offered: microfiche; 16mm and 35mm microfilm
Micropublication programs: Microfilming of documents dating from the
    eleventh to the twentieth centuries, which form the surviving archives of
    central government in England and Wales and later in the United Kingdom.
    These records include Foreign Office Records; U.S.A. Embassy
    Correspondence and Colonial Office Records.

PUBLICATIONS GERARD MONFORT
Saint-Pierre-de-Salerne, 27800 Brionne France

Microformats offered: microfiche
Micropublication programs: Monographs on European culture and history,
    political science and sociology.

PUBLICATIONS ORIENTALISTES DE FRANCE, a Division of Institut
  National des Langues et des Civilisation Orientales
4, rue de Lille, 75007 Paris, France

Tel: 260-67-05
Cable Address: PUBOR PARIS
General Manager: Simone Sieffert
Promotion Manager/Customer Service: Françoise Thiriet
Microformats offered: microfiche
Micropublication programs: Black Africa, 1500-1910; Japan, 1500-1910; Viet-
  Nam; Indonesia until 1910; Persia; Former Ecole Nationale des Langues
  Orientales Vivantes publications.

READEX MICROPRINT CORP.
101 Fifth Ave., New York, NY 10003

Tel: 212/243-3822
Board Chairman: Albert Boni
President: William F. Boni
Product Manager: K. K. Miklas
Treasurer: Miriam M. Apsel
Microformats offered: micro-opaque cards
Micropublication programs: The basic aim of the Readex micropublishing
  program today is that established by founder, Albert Boni: To make
  available to libraries in microform research and reference material which
  would be (a) too costly or (b) inaccessible in conventional format. Programs
  include: Early American Imprints, Early American Newspapers, Landmarks
  of Science, Government Documents.

THE REGENTS PRESS OF KANSAS
366 Watson Library, Lawrence, KS 66045

Director: John H. Langley
Microformats offered: microfiche
Micropublication programs: Foreign-Language Units of Kansas.

RESEARCH PUBLICATIONS, INC.
12 Lunar Dr., Woodbridge, CT 06525

Tel: 203/397-2600
Chairman: Samuel B. Freedman
President: Milton Mandel
Director of Marketing: Paul Ferster
Microformats offered: microfiche; 16mm and 35mm microfilm
Micropublication programs: Research Publications specializes in making
    available subject collections of research material for scholarship and
    industry. Access is provided through prepared bibliography-indexes,
    cataloguing and film targets.

THE ROCKEFELLER UNIVERSITY PRESS
1230 York Avenue, New York, NY 10021

Tel: 212/360-1278
Manager, Journals Office: Margaret Broadbent
Microformats offered: microfiche; 16mm and 35mm microfilm
Micropublication programs: To provide availability in microform of the back
    files from Volume 1 of Biophysical Journal, The Journal of Cell Biology, The
    Journal of Clinical Investigation, The Journal of Experimental Medicine and
    The Journal of General Physiology. Delivery to current subscribers is
    speeded by simultaneous microfiche and hard copy publication.

FRANKLIN D. ROOSEVELT LIBRARY
Albany Post Rd., Hyde Park, NY 12538

Tel: 914/229-8114
Director: William R. Emerson
Microformats offered: 35mm microfilm
Micropublication programs: The Press Conferences of Franklin D. Roosevelt
    1933-1945; A Comprehensive Index to the Press Conferences of Franklin
    D. Roosevelt 1933-1945; The Messages between Franklin D. Roosevelt
    and Winston S. Churchill 1939-1945; Papers of Henry A. Wallace 1940-44.

FRED B. ROTHMAN & CO.
57 Leuning St., South Hackensack, NJ 07606

Tel: 201/489-4646
President: Fred B. Rothman
Vice President: Paul A. Rothman
Microformats offered: microfiche; 16mm and 35mm microfilm
Micropublication programs: Back files of journals, monographs, and
government documents in law and related fields.

SCHEFFEL'SCHE VERLAGSBUCHHANDLUNG
Berghausener Strasse 21, D-4018 Langenfeld, West Germany

Publisher: Walter Scheffel
Microformats offered: microfiche
Micropublication programs: Microedition of a journal devoted to
micrographics—Microdok.

SCHIERENBERG, DIETER B.V.
Amsteldijk 44, Amsterdam, The Netherlands

Tel: 020-769280
Telex: 15798 jbds
Cable Address: Natper
Director: Dieter Schierenberg
Microformats offered: microfiche
Micropublication programs: Palaeontologia Indica (old series and new series);
Palaeontologia Sinica (old series and new series); Southern Tibet Discoveries.
by Sven Hedin; Acta Palaeontologia Sinica; Fauna and Flora des Golfes der
Neapel und der angr Meeresabschnittel Fauna e Flora del golfo di Napoli.

SCHNASE MICROFILM SYSTEMS
120 Brown Rd., Scarsdale, NY 10583

Tel: 914/725-1284
Cable Address: Schnasbook
Owner: Mrs. Annemarie Schnase
Asst. Manager: Mrs. Gisela Kretschmann
Microformats offered: 35mm microfilm
Micropublication programs: Music periodicals; Academy publications.

SCHOLARLY RESOURCES, INC.
1508 Pennsylvania Avenue, Wilmington, DE 19806

Tel: 302/654-7713
President: T. Wistar Brown IV
Vice President: Daniel C. Helmstadter
Treasurer: Dale H. Zentz
Production Manager: James L. Preston
Chief Research Editor: Helen Cripe
Microformats offered: microfiche; 35mm microfilm
Micropublication programs: Primary source materials on 35mm microfilm and
microfiche in the humanities and social sciences for college, university and
research libraries.

SCHOLARS' FACSIMILIES & REPRINTS
P.O. Box 344, Delmar, NY 12054

Tel: 518/439-6146
General Editor: Norman Mangouni
Microformats offered: microfiche
Micropublication programs: Limited editions of rare or out-of-print books of
interest to scholars. These are facsimile re-editions with introductory essays
giving provenance of the works and relevant biographical, bibliographical,
or critical information.

SCOLAR PRESS LTD.
39 Great Russell St., London WC1B 3PH England

Tel: 01-636-1865
Chairman: J. E. Commander
Sales Manager: Hallam Murray
Microformats offered: microfiche
Micropublication programs: English Linguistics.

SERVICE INTERNATIONAL DE MICROFILMS
9 rue Du Commandant Riviere, Paris 8, France

Tel: 359-16-31
Director: William Hawkins
Microformats offered: 35mm microfilm
Micropublication programs: Journals and newspapers; Statistique de la
    France; Le Tite-Live de Charles V. Appointed microfilmers for nineteen
    Parisian special libraries (Humanities) and for the reproduction of
    Diplomatic Archives of the French Foreign Ministry; charged with special
    programs at the French National Archives.

BARRY SHURLOCK & CO. (PUBLISHERS) LTD.
174 Stockbridge Road, Winchester Hants, 5022 6RW England

Tel: 0962-67030
Managing Director: E. M. Shurlock
Microformats offered: microfiche
Micropublication programs: The Book of the Farm.

SIAM (Society for Industrial and Applied Mathematics)
33 South 17th Street, Philadelphia, PA 19103

Tel: 215/564-2929
Managing Director: I. Edward Block
Marketing Manager: Hugh B. Hair
Customer Service: Eloise Holman
Microformats offered: 16mm and 35mm microfilm
Micropublication programs: The fundamental literature of applied
    mathematics including: SIAM Journal on Applied Mathematics, SIAM
    Journal on Computing, SIAM Journal on Control and Optimization, SIAM
    Journal on Mathematical Analysis, SIAM Journal on Numerical Analysis,
    SIAM Review, Theory of Probability and Its Applications.

SIBLEY MUSIC LIBRARY MICROFORM SERVICE
44 Swan St., Rochester, NY 14604

Tel: 716/275-3018
Head Librarian: Dr. Ruth Watanabe
Associate Librarian: Charles Lindahl
Circulation Librarian and Micrographic Specialist: Stuart Milligan
Microformats offered: microfiche; micro-opaque cards; 16mm and 35mm
   microfilm
Micropublication programs: Early music literature reproduced from originals at
   the Library of Congress and at the Sibley Music Library of the Eastman
   School of Music of the University of Rochester (formerly marketed under the
   name of The University of Rochester Press); Eastman School of Music
   theses and dissertations which have not been marketed by Xerox University
   Microfilms; on-demand requests for public domain materials including
   music, theoretical treatises, music periodicals etc.

SIMON FRASER UNIVERSITY
Office of the University Librarian, Burnaby 2, British Columbia, Canada

Tel: 604/291-3261
Telex: 04-53449
Microformats offered: 35mm microfilm
Micropublication programs: Early Canadian Periodicals on Microfilm.

SOCIETY OF AUTOMOTIVE ENGINEERS, INC.
400 Commonwealth Dr., Warrendale, PA 15096

Tel: 412/776-4841
Telex: 886355
Marketing Manager, Publications: R. A. Morris
Microformats offered: microfiche
Micropublication programs: The Society provides microfiche of their entire
   publications output each year-approximately 700 technical papers and ten
   books.

SOCIETY OF EXPLORATION GEOPHYSICISTS
3707 E. 51 St., Tulsa, OK 74135

Tel: 918/743-1365
Microformats offered: micro-opaque cards
Micropublication programs: Geophysics.

SOMERSET HOUSE
417 Maitland Avenue, Teaneck, NJ 07666

Tel: 201/833-1795
President: Peter Kurz
Distributor for: Chadwyck-Healey Ltd.
Microformats offered: microfiche (including color); 35mm microfilm (including
    color)
Micropublication programs: Art exhibition catalogs on microfiche, European
    and World official statistical serials on microfiche, Archives of British and
    American publishers on microfiche, BBC daily radio news on microfiche,
    government publications on microform, Index of American Design on color
    microfiche.

SOUTH CAROLINA DEPARTMENT OF ARCHIVES AND HISTORY
1430 Senate St., P.O. Box 11,669, Capitol Station, Columbia, SC 29211

Tel: 803/758-5816
Editor: Judith M. Brimelow
Microformats offered: 35mm microfilm
Micropublication programs: Records in the British Public Record Office
    relating to South Carolina, 1663-1782; Records of the Public Treasurers of
    South Carolina, 1725-1776; Duties on Trade at Charleston, 1784-1789;
    Records of the South Carolina Treasury, 1775-1780, 1783-1791, 1791-
    1865; Agriculture, Industry, Social Statistics, and Mortality Schedules for
    South Carolina, 1850-1880; Accounts Audited of Claims growing out of the
    Revolution in South Carolina (in progress—A-R completed), Editor: Judith
    M. Brimelow: County Records on Microfilm: contact publisher for complete
    listings.

THE SOUTHERN BAPTIST CONVENTION HISTORICAL COMMISSION
127 Ninth Ave., North, Nashville, TN 37234

Tel: 615/251-2660
Executive Director: Lynn E. May, Jr.
Assistant Executive Director: A. Ronald Tonks
Microfilm Secretary: Kathy Grenga
Microformats offered: 16mm and 35mm microfilm
Micropublication programs: Books, periodicals, newspapers, pamphlets,
    manuscripts, archival materials, records of local churches, records of
    denominational bodies, and other materials by or about Baptists in the USA
    and around the world. Materials on microfilm total over 10,000,000 pages of
    Baptistiana.

SOUTHERN ILLINOIS UNIVERSITY PRESS
P.O. Box 3697, Carbondale, IL 62901

Tel: 618/453-2281-2
Microformats offered: microfiche
Micropublication programs: Micropublication of Concordance to Joseph
    Conrad's Heart of Darkness.

SPRINGER-VERLAG NEW YORK INC.
175 Fifth Avenue, New York, NY 10010

Tel: 212/673-2660
President: Dr. H. Goetze
Executive Vice-President & CEO: Bernd Grossmann
Treasurer, Vice-President: Bernard Brouder
Secretary: Victor Borsodi
Director of Marketing, Vice-President: Robert G. Dundas
Journal & Microedition Sales Services: Inge Valentine
Microformats offered: microfiche; 16mm and 35mm microfilm
Micropublication programs: Archive for Rational Mechanics and Analysis;
    Communications in Mathematical Physics; Numerische Mathematik;
    Psychopharmacologia; Theoretica Chimica Acta; Zentralblatt fuer
    Mathematik, et al.

THE STANFORD UNIVERSITY LIBRARIES
Special Collections, Stanford, CA 94305

Tel: 415/321-2300
Manuscripts Librarian: Patricia J. Palmer
Microformats offered: 35mm microfilm
Micropublication programs: The Francis B. Loomis Papers 1835-1959:
   William R. Shafter Papers 1862-1938.

STATE HISTORICAL SOCIETY OF COLORADO
1300 Broadway, Denver, CO 80203

Tel: 303/839-2305
Curator of Documentary Resources: Maxine Benson
Microformats offered: 35mm microfilm
Micropublication programs: Microfilming current Colorado newspapers from
   all areas of the state.

STATE HISTORICAL SOCIETY OF WISCONSIN
Library, 816 State St., Madison, WI 53706

Tel: 608/262-9583
Sales: James Buckett
Microformats offered: 35mm microfilm
Micropublication programs: Programs consist of microfilming materials for the
   Society's collection, with sales as a by-product. Emphasis is on labor and
   Wisconsin.

STATE UNIVERSITY OF NEW YORK PRESS
99 Washington Ave., Albany, NY 12210

Tel: 518/474-6050
Director: Norman Mangouni
Adv. and Promotion: Elnora Carrino
Microformats offered: microfiche
Micropublication programs: Original monographs.

SWETS & ZEITLINGER B.V.
Weereweg 347b, Lisse, The Netherlands

Tel: 02521-19113
Telex: 41.32.5
Microformats offered: 16mm and 35mm microfilm
Micropublication programs: Periodicals.

TAYLOR AND FRANCIS LTD.
10-14 Macklin St., London WC2B 5NF England

Tel: 01-405-2237/9
Microformats offered: microfiche
Micropublication programs: Back issues of the publisher's international
    scientific journals.

TEMPLE UNIVERSITY SCHOOL OF LAW
Charles Klein Library, 1715 N. Broad St., Philadelphia, PA 19122

Tel: 215/787-7891
Law Librarian: Erwin C. Surrency
Microformats offered: 35mm microfilm
Micropublication programs: Publications of the Sections and House of
    Delegates of the American Bar Association; American Law Record;
    Jurisprudent; Pennsylvania Law Series; U.S. Monthly Law Magazine;
    Blackstone's Commentaries.

3M COMPANY
Library Systems, Box 33600, St. Paul, MN 55133

Tel: 612/733-1186
Manager: Dr. Graham Gurr
Microformats offered: microfiche
Micropublication programs: The 3M Bibliographic Control System provides
    MARC (Machine Readable Cataloging) and non-MARC cataloging of the
    Library of Congress. Also North American Shared cataloging is offered.

TIME SHARE CORPORATION, MICROPUBLISHING
3 Lebanon St., Hanover, NH 03755

Tel: 603/643-3640
President: Richard T. Bueschel
Micropublishing Manager: James N. Taylor
Microformats offered: microfiche
Micropublication programs: The National College Catalog Service (NCCS) is a
  microfiche file containing approximately 1500 college catalogs from four-
  year institutions.

TRANS-MEDIA, A Division of Chas. H. Bohn & Co., Inc.
  A Member of the Oceana Group
75 Main St., Dobbs Ferry, NY 10522

Tel: 914/693-5956
President: Philip F. Cohen
Vice Presidents: David R. Cohen, Anne Loscalzo
Editorial & Administrative: Edwin S. Newman
Microformats offered: microfiche; 35mm microfilm
Micropublication programs: An integrated program of legal publication in
  microform—American, British and International—including State Reports,
  Code of Federal Regulations, Attorneys-General Opinions, Bar Association
  Proceedings; English, Irish and Scottish nominatives; UN Treaty Series and
  materials. Also parliamentary publications; Economics Working Papers.

TRIGON PRESS
117 Kent House Road, Beckenham Kent BR3 1JJ, England

Tel: 01-778-0534
Directors: Roger and Judith Sheppard
Microformats offered: microfiche (including color)
Micropublication programs: OP books for the book trade. Developing
  programme on auction prices for rare books 1930-1940. Other projects
  include medieval alphabets, lettering and manuscript writing on fiche.

TUSKEGEE INSTITUTE, DIVISION OF BEHAVIORAL SCIENCE
RESEARCH
Tuskegee Institute, AL 36088

Tel: 205/727-8575
Director: Paul L. Wall
Customer Service: Celia Jefferson
Microformats offered: 35mm microfilm
Micropublication programs: Microfilm Publication of the George Washington
Carver Papers (1864-1943) at Tuskegee Institute; Microfilm Publication of
the Newspaper Clipping File (1898-1966) at Tuskegee Institute (Race
Relations in the South).

TV GUIDE
Radnor, PA 19088

Tel: 215/688-7400
Microfilm Representative: Cathy Johnson
Microformats offered: 35mm microfilm
Micropublication programs: Back issues of TV Guide, all editions.

UNIFO PUBLISHERS LTD.
P.O. Box 89, White Plains, NY 10602

Tel: 914/592-8710
Director: John A. Burn
Microformats offered: microfiche
Micropublication programs: Documentation of International Governmental
Organizations with emphasis on the United Nations. Also Agents for all UN
Publications—Microforms and Printed Editions.

UNITED NATIONS
(Publications Section) Room LX 2300, New York, NY 10017

Tel: 212/754-1234
Cable Address: UNATIONS NEW YORK
Chief, Sales Section: W. Scott Laing
Marketing Manager: Bjorn Hafgren
Operations Manager: Charles H. Hall
Sales Officer: David Griffin
Microformats offered: microfiche; 35mm microfilm
Micropublication programs: United Nations Treaty Series: General Assembly
    Official Records; Security Council Official Records; Economic and Social
    Council Official Records; Trusteeship Council Official Records; Includes
    Yearbooks on: United Nations, International Statistics, Demography,
    Human Rights, National Accounts Statistics, International Trade Statistics,
    Juridical and Trade Law.

UNITED STATES GOVERNMENT PRINTING OFFICE
Washington, DC 20402

Tel: 202/275-3345
Assistant Public Printer: C. A. LaBarre
Microformats offered: microfiche
Micropublication programs: Government documents.

THE UNITED STATES HISTORICAL DOCUMENTS INSTITUTE
1911 Fort Myer Drive, Arlington, VA 22209

Tel: 703/525-6035
Chairman: Franklin D. Crawford
President: William W. Buchanan
Microformats offered: microfiche; 16mm and 35mm microfilm
Micropublication programs: Proceedings of the U.S. Congress; Canadian
    Parliamentary Proceedings & Sessional Papers; Her Majesty's Stationery
    Office Publications; Transportation Masterfile.

U.S. NATIONAL ARCHIVES AND RECORDS SERVICE
Publications Sales Branch, Washington, DC 20408

Tel: 202/523-3181
Chief, Publication Sales Branch: Wilbur Valentine
Microformats offered: 35mm microfilm
Micropublication programs: Microfilming United States historical documents and archives.

UNIVELT INC.
P.O. Box 28130, San Diego, CA 92128

Tel: 714/746-4005 or 714/487-7560
President: H. Jacobs
Microformats offered: microfiche; 35mm microfilm
Micropublication programs: Micropublishes proceedings of professional associations on microfiche, especially technical proceedings. Provides consulting services to such associations in developing their microform programs.

UNIVERSITY MICROFILMS INTERNATIONAL
300 North Zeeb Road, Ann Arbor, MI 48106

Tel: 313/761-4700
Telex: 0235569
President: Joseph J. Fitzsimmons
Vice-President, Editorial Services: Stevens Rice
Vice-President and General Manager for Books & Collections: Sheldon Kramer
Vice-President and General Manager for Dissertations: Helen Greenway
Vice-President and General Manager for Serials: Douglas Norman
Vice-President and General Manager for Western Hemisphere Sales: Jim Gilligan
Microformats offered: microfiche; 16mm and 35mm microfilm (including color)
Micropublication programs: Information produced on demand from books, periodicals, manuscripts—new and old, doctoral dissertations and research reports, government documents and significant newspapers—all in a form most suitable for use in libraries: lithographic printing, xerographic printing, or microfilm.

UNIVERSITY MICROFILMS LIMITED
18 Bedford Row, London WC1R 4EJ, England

Tel: 01-242-9485
Telex: 8811363 EXEL G
Managing Director: Robert Simpson
Sales Development Manager: John Hodder
Micorformats offered: microfiche (including color); 16mm and 35mm microfilm
(including color)
Micropublication programs: Serials in Microform, Doctoral Dissertations,
Books on Demand, Special Collections and Monographs.

UNIVERSITY MUSIC EDITIONS, a Division of High Density Systems, Inc.
P.O. Box 192, Fort George Station, NY 10040

Tel: 212/569-5393/5340
Vice President: Christopher Pavlakis
Technology: Donald Leinbach
Microformats offered: microfiche
Micropublication programs: Publications of music and music literature:
complete works of master composers, anthologies, monuments of music,
histories, dictionaries, journals, treatises, bibliographies, monographs,
special unique collections.

THE UNIVERSITY OF CHICAGO PRESS
5801 Ellis Ave., Chicago, IL 60637

Tel: 312/753-2564
Telex: 25-4603
Cable Address: UNIPRESSCGO
Director: Morris Philipson
Managing Editor, Text-Fiche Program: Wendy J. Strothman
Microformats offered: microfiche (including color)
Micropublication programs: Color and black and white illustrations of art,
artifacts, and archival photographs from museum collections reproduced on
microfiche and combined with conventional text—all scholarly publications.

UNIVERSITY OF IOWA
Libraries, Iowa City, IA 52242

Tel: 319/353-4450
Microformats offered: 35mm microfilm
Micropublication programs: The Papers of Henry A. Wallace.

UNIVERSITY OF LONDON, INSTITUTE OF UNITED STATES STUDIES
31 Tavistock Square, London WC1H 9EZ, England

Director: Professor Esmond Wright
Bibliographer: Angela Smith
Microformats offered: microfiche
Micropublication programs: A comprehensive bibliography of American
    Studies books selected from worldwide sources. Non-cumulating lists are
    produced monthly and the lists are cumulated at the end of each year in an
    Annual Cumulation.

UNIVERSITY OF OREGON, College of Health, Physical Education and
    Recreation
Eugene, OR 97403

Tel: 503/686-4117
Executive Director: Dr. Jan Broekhoff
Administrative Assistant: Mrs. Wanda Hickson
Microformats offered: microfiche
Micropublication programs: Unpublished research materials in health,
    physical education, recreation and dance which have national significance,
    particularly doctoral dissertations and masters' theses, as well as scholarly
    books and journals now out-of-print.

UNIVERSITY OF QUEENSLAND PRESS MICROFORM DIVISION
P.O. Box 42, St. Lucia, Qld., 4067 Australia

Tel: 3706291 (Brisbane)
Telex: UNIPRESS
Cable Address: AA40315
Manager: Frank Thompson
Microform Editor: Craig Munro
Microformats offered: 35mm microfilm
Micropublication programs: The University of Queensland Press Microform
   Division was established to help disseminate important research material,
   principally relating to Australia (and including Paupa New Guinea).

UNIVERSITY OF TORONTO PRESS
St. George Campus, Toronto, Ont. M5S 1A6 Canada

Tel: 416/978-2239
Director: Marsh Jeanneret
Microformats offered: microfiche
Micropublication programs: Original monographs on microfiche.

UNIVERSITY OF WASHINGTON PRESS
Seattle, WA 98195

Tel: 206/543-4050
Director: Donald R. Ellegood
Non-Print Media: Ott H. Hyatt
Microformats offered: microfiche
Micropublication programs: All books are offered in microfiche editions.
   Original microfiche Series—Nineteenth-Century Popular British Drama.

UNIVERSITY PUBLICATIONS OF AMERICA, INC.
5630 Connecticut Avenue, Washington, DC 20015

Tel: 202/362-6201
President: John Moscato
Editor: Paul Kesaris
Research Editors: Mark Fox, Joan Hardesty, Michael Moscato
Sales Department: Anthony Houser, Barbara Lowitz
Production Department: Luis Munoz, Frances Lavery, Sandy Bryll-Quist,
    Mark Egan, Brian McLaughlin
Microformats offered: 35mm microfilm
Micropublication programs: Publishers of major archival collections and
    research projects which serve the academic needs of the scholars of today
    and tomorrow.

UPDATA PUBLIATIONS, INC.
1756 Westwood Blvd., Los Angeles, CA 90024

Tel: 213/474-5900
President: Herbert Sclar
Vice President: Gina Ellen
International Sales: Jim Butchywood
Customer Service: Jo Ann Wolff
Microformats offered: microfiche
Micropublication programs: Research and Development documents for
    special libraries in aeronautics, mining, metallurgy, and energy. Updata
    offers individual microfiche on demand to complete collections.

VERLAG DOKUMENTATION, PUBLISHERS
P.O. Box 711009, Pössenbacherstr. 2, 8000 München 71, Federal Republic
    of Germany

Tel: (089) 798901
Telex: 5212067
Microformats offered: microfiche
Micropublication programs: Marburger Index, 500,000 photographs on the
    fine arts in Germany contained in the Bildarchiv Foto Marburg and the
    Rheinisches Bildarchiv in Cologne.

WEST PUBLISHING COMPANY
50 W. Kellogg, P.O. Box 3526, St. Paul, MN 55165

Tel: 612/228-2971
Microform Development: Robert F. Hajicek
Microformats offered: microfiche; ultramicrofiche
Micropublication programs: National Reporter System, First series in
   Ultrafiche: Federal Reporter, Pacific Reporter, North Eastern Reporter,
   Atlantic Reporter, North Western Reporter, South Western Reporter,
   Southern Reporter, South Eastern Reporter, New York Supplement.
   Second series in Ultrafiche: Federal Reporter Vols. 1-150.

J. WHITAKER & SONS, LTD.
12 Dyott Street, London, WC1, England

Tel: 01-637-1105
Cable Address: Whitmanack, London W.C.1.
Microformats offered: microfiche
Micropublication programs: British Books in Print, monthly, records with full
   details under author, title and subject, all books available for sale in the
   United Kingdom.

JAMES T. WHITE AND COMPANY
1700 State Highay Three, Clifton, NJ 07013

Tel: 201/773-9300
President: William H. White
Editor-in-Chief: Raymond D. McGill
Microformats offered: microfiche
Micropublication programs: National Cyclopedia of American Biography; The
   Papers of Benjamin Henry Latrobe.

WILDLIFE DISEASE ASSOCIATION
P.O. Box 886, Ames, IA 50010

Tel: 512/232-1433
President: William G. Winkler DVM
Vice President: Joan Budd DVM
Treasurer: Leslie A. Page PhD
Microformats offered: microfiche (including color); micro-opaque cards
Micropublication programs: Journal of Wildlife Diseases.

WILEY-INTERSCIENCE JOURNALS
John Wiley & Sons, Inc., 605 Third Ave., New York, NY 10016

Tel: 212/867-9800
Journals Manager: Allan Wittman
Microformats offered: microfiche; 16mm and 35mm microfilm
Micropublication programs: Wiley scientific and technical journals are
available in microform three months after end of calendar year volume,
starting with volume one for each journal.

THE WILLIAMS & WILKINS CO.
428 E. Preston St., Baltimore, MD 21202

Tel: 301/528-4249
Telex: 8-7669
Cable Address: Wilco Baltimore
Microfilm Sales: Joan B. Schuman
Microformats offered: 16mm and 35mm microfilm
Micropublication programs: Medical, scientific and technical journals.

WOMEN'S HISTORY RESEARCH CENTER
2325 Oak St., Berkeley, CA 94708

Tel: 415/548-1770
Director: Laura X
Microformats offered: 35mm microfilm
Micropublication programs: Women and Law and Women and Health/Mental
Health are topical collections of vertical file materials. Herstory is a collection
of women's periodicals from 1956-1974.

WORLD MICROFILMS PUBLICATIONS LTD.
62 Queen's Grove, London NW8 6ER, England

Tel: 01-586-3092
Cable Address: Microworld London NW8
Director: S. C. Albert
Technical Information: Mike Gunn
Microformats offered: microfiche; 35mm microfilm (including color)
Micropublication programs: Research Collections in Microform, Reprints of
Periodicals in Microform. Major Programmes include Medieval
Manuscripts, Labour History, Cinema Studies, Architectural Studies,
Photographic Studies, American/Canadian Studies, etc.

YALE UNIVERSITY LIBRARY
Publications Office, New Haven, CT 06520

Tel: 203/436-8335
Administrator: Mary Ellen Moore
Microformats offered: 16mm and 35mm microfilm
Micropublication programs: The Publications Office handles sales for
   microform reproductions of certain Library materials, notably the Catalog,
   Yale Ph.D dissertations, and material filmed for preservation purposes.

YUSHODO FILM PUBLICATIONS, LTD.
29 Saneicho, Shinjuku-ku, Tokyo, Japan

Tel: 03-357-1411
Managing Director: Yuji Nitta
General Manager: Katsuyuki Yokoyama
Microformats offered: 35mm microfilm
Micropublication programs: Special collections of Japanese literature,
   historical records, laws, government documents and newspapers.

LOST CAUSE PRESS
750-56 Starks Building
LOUISVILLE, KENTUCKY
40202

LIST OF MICROFICHE PUBLICATIONS

Selected volumes from	Volumes	Price
1. *American Fiction 1774-1900* Lyle H. Wright	3289	$28,479.00*
2. *19th Century American Literature and History*		
The Ohio Valley The South	1401	10,473.00
The Trans-Mississippi West	2135	15,997.00*
3. *Travels in the West & Southwest*	500	3,750.00
4. *Afro-American Studies Materials*	5000	48,960.00
"The most comprehensive corpus of material available in this field."		
5. *British Culture,* Series One/18th and 19th Century	848	5,947.00
Contemporary and retrospective history, biography, and criticism of 18th century English literature. Victorian Prose, Critical and Miscellaneous. Reference Works and Collections.		
6. *British Culture,* Series Two	1035	7,762.00*
Selected volumes from *The New Cambridge Bibliography of English Literature,* Volume 3, 1800-1900 (1969), edited by George Watson.		
7. *Selected Americana from Sabin's Dictionary of Books Relating to America from Its Discovery to the Present Time*	6330	67,297.00*
8. *The Kentucky Culture Series* A Basic Library of Kentuckiana	2311	16,785.00*
9. *Kentucky Thousand*	1073	7,500.00
10. *A Miscellany*	106	682.00
Rare and esoteric works of great importance to libraries.		
11. *The Plains and The Rockies* H. R. Wagner and C. L. Camp	537	10,000.00
12. *Anti-Slavery Propaganda Collection* Oberlin College Library	2500	17,671.00

LOST CAUSE PRESS

750-56 Starks Building

LOUISVILLE, KENTUCKY

40202

LIST OF MICROFICHE PUBLICATIONS

Selected volumes from	Volumes	Price
13. *Slavery. Source Material and Critical Literature*	1588	11,909.00*
Selections from *A Bibliography of American Slavery.* Dwight L. Dumond and *The Library of Congress Collection.* Continuing by subscription.		
14. *Travels in the Confederate States* E. M. Coulter	448	6,687.00
15. *Travels in the New South I & II* Thomas D. Clark	611	6,642.00
16. *Travels in the Old South I, II, III* Thomas D. Clark	1174	16,593.00
17. *Western Americana*	1328	9,960.00
18. *The Literature of Theology and Church History*	500	4,500.00*
19. *Harleian Miscellany*	12	180.00
20. *The Parker Society*	55	615.00
21. *Somers Tracts*	13	260.00

PLEASE WRITE OR CALL COLLECT TO NANCY OR BURREL FARNSLEY FOR DESCRIPTIVE CATALOGS AND TITLE LISTS. AREA CODE 502/584-8404.

All collections listed are in print.

Each collection in print complete with a full set of catalog cards.

Duplicates of items already in library collections may be returned for full credit within six months of receipt of shipment.

*These collections are ongoing projects and we deliver from 200 to 600 new titles per year to subscribers at a special standing order price. A standing order may be cancelled at any time.

Payments and delivery of collections in print may be arranged in any of the following ways: (a) delivery of the full microfiche collection (b) delivery of the full microfiche collection with payment spread over several years (c) delivery of a portion of the collection each year for several years with payment made only for the portion received. Under purchase arrangement "(c)" an order may be cancelled at any time.

MANSELL MICROFORMS

Archives of British Men of Science
By Roy M. MacLeod and James R. Friday
65 fiches (COSATI 60 frame format) plus printed index and guide, binder, £65.00/U.S.$108.00

The Brasenose Conference on the Automation of Libraries
Edited by John Harrison and Peter Laslett
2 fiches (NMA 98 frame format), £3.00/U.S.$5.00

John Tyndall, Natural Philosopher, 1820-1893: Catalogue of Correspondence, Journals and Collected Papers
By James R. Friday, Roy M. MacLeod and Philippa Shepherd
34 fiches (COSATI 60 frame format) plus printed index and guide, binder, £40.00/U.S.$66.00

Letter-Books of Charles M. Blomfield, Bishop of London, in Lambeth Palace Library, 1828-1855
207 fiches (COSATI 60 frame format), £250.00/U.S.$425.00

The Process Books of the Court of Arches at Lambeth Palace Library 1660-1893
Executive editor: Melanie Barber
abt. 2,000 fiches per annum (COSATI 60 frame format), prices on request

Studies in Maritime History
By Charles H. Cotter
• **Volume 1**, A History of Nautical Astronomical Tables
(10 fiches), £20.00/U.S.$34.50
• **Volume 2**, A History of Ship Magnetism
(9 fiches), £18.00/U.S.$31.00
• **Volume 3**, A Pathway to Perfect Sailing: A History of Dead Reckoning Navigation *(6 fiches), £12.00/U.S.$21.00*
NMA 98 frame format fiches, also available as a set with binder, £42.50/U.S.$73.00

Union Catalogue of Scientific Libraries in the University of Cambridge, Books published before 1801
9 fiches (COSATI 60 frame format), binder, £12.50/U.S.$21.50

Prices subject to VAT in U.K.

Please write for a complete list of microform publications

 **Mansell**

3 BLOOMSBURY PLACE LONDON WC1A 2QA ENGLAND

The following organizations do not market micropublications, but will microfilm their holdings on request. These organizations are largely university and national library reprographic centers. Acknowledgement is given to Joseph Z. Nitecki, editor of the *Directory of Library Reprographic Services* for permission to list this information.

ALABAMA

Alabama Department of Archives
and History
624 Washington Avenue
Montgomery, Alabama 36130

Alabama Public Library Service
State of Alabama
Montgomery, Alabama 36130

Auburn University
Interlibrary Loans
Ralph Brown Draughon Library
Auburn, Alabama 36830
TWX: 810-744-3020
NUC Code: AAP

Jacksonville State University
Interlibrary Loan
Jacksonville, Alabama, 36265

Samford University Library
Microfilm Department
Birmingham, Alabama 35209
NUC Code: ABH

Troy State University
The Library
Troy, Alabama 36081

University of Alabama Library
Interlibrary Loans Service
University, Alabama 35486
TWX: 810-729-5845
NUC Code: AU

University of Alabama in
Birmingham
Interlibrary Loan Service
Mervyn H. Sterne Library
University College
University Station
Birmingham, Alabama 35294

ALASKA

Alaska Division of State Libraries
and Museums
(Alaska Department of Education)
Pouch G
Juneau, Alaska 99811

University of Alaska, Anchorage
Interlibrary Loans
3211 Providence Drive
Anchorage, Alaska 99504

The Elmer E. Rasmuson Library
University of Alaska, Fairbanks
Fairbanks, Alaska 99701
Telex: 35429
NUC Code: AkU

Arkansas State University
Interlibrary Loan Department
Dean B. Ellis Library
State University, Arkansas 72467
Telex/TWX: 910-728-6507
ARSTU LIB JONE
NUC Code: ArStC

John Brown University
Library
Siloam Springs, Arizona 72761

ARIZONA

Arizona State University Library
Interlibrary Loan Service
Tempe, Arizona 85281
TWX: 910-950-4693
 NUC Code: Aztes

 Department of Library, Archives
and Public Records
3rd Floor State Capitol
Phoenix, Arizona 85007
TWX: 910-950-0145

 Northern Arizona University
Libraries
Interlibrary Loans
Flagstaff, Arizona 86011
TWX: 910-972-0964
 NUC Code: AzFU

University of Arizona Library
Interlibrary Loan
Tucson, Arizona 85721
TWX: 910-952-1143
NUC Code: AZU

ARKANSAS

Arkansas Library Commission
506 ½ Center Street
Little Rock, Arkansas 72201

University of Arkansas
Interlibrary Loans
University Libraries
Fayetteville, Arkansas 72701
TWX: 910-720-6666
NUC Code: ArU

University of Arkansas at Little
Rock Library
33rd and University
Little Rock, Arkansas, 72204

CALIFORNIA

California Institute of Technology
Interlibrary Loan
Millikan Memorial Library 1-32
Pasadena, California 91125
NUC Code: CPT

California State University, Fresno
The Library
Fresno, California 93740
NUC Code: CFS

California State University,
Fullerton
Library-Interlibrary Loan
Subsection
Box 4150
Fullerton, California 92634
NUC Code: CFIs

California State University,
Long Beach
The Library
1250 Bellflower Blvd.
Long Beach, California 90840
TWX: 910-341-7654

California State University,
Sacramento
The Library, Circulation Department
6000 J Street
Sacramento, California 95819

Section II

REPROGRAPHIC CENTERS

Claremont Colleges
Honnold Library
Interlibrary Loans
Claremont, California 91711
NUC Code: CCC

Hoover Institution
Photographic Service
Reference Department
Stanford, California 94305
NUC Code: CSt-H

Huntington Library, Art Gallery &
Botanical Gardens
1151 Oxford Road
San Marino, California 91108
NUC Code: CSMH

Loma Linda University Library
Loma Linda, California 92354
And:
Loma Linda University Library
Riverside, California 92505
TWX: 910-332-1314

San Diego Public Library
820 E Street
San Diego, California 92101
TWX: 910-335-2043
NUC Code: CSd

San Diego State University
Malcolm A. Love Library
Interlibrary Loans
San Diego, California 92182
TWX: 910-335-1565
NUC Code: CSdS

San Francisco Public Library
Larkin & McAllister Streets
San Francisco, California 94102

San Francisco State University
Library Rapid Copy Service /ILL
San Francisco, California 94132

Stanford University Libraries
Interlibrary Loan Service
Stanford, California 94305
TWX: 910-373-1787
NUC Code: CSt

University of California
Interlibrary Loan Department
(Photoduplication Section)
The General Library
Berkeley, California 94720
TWX: 910-366-7337
NUC Codes: CU (for General Library)
CU-B (for the Bancroft Library)

University of California
Interlibrary Loan Service
Shields Library
Davis, California 95616
TWX: 910-367-2071
NUC Code: CU-A

University of California, Irvine
Interlibrary Loan Service
General Library
P.O. Box 19557
Irvine, California 92713
TWX: 910-595-1770
NUC Code: CU-I

University of California, Los Angeles
Library A-V and Photoservices
6 Powell Library
405 Hilgard Avenue
Los Angeles, California 90024
TWX: 910-342-6973
NUC Code: CLU

University of California Library
Interlibrary Loans
P.O. Box 5900
Riverside, California 92507
NUC Code: CU-Riv

University of California, San Diego
Interlibrary Loans
The University Library
La Jolla, California 92093
TWX: 910-337-1777 and
910-337-1279 (bio-medical requests)
NUC Code: CU-S

University of California, San Francisco
The Library
San Francisco, California 94143
NUC Code: CU-M

University of California, Santa Barbara
Library
Interlibrary Loan
Santa Barbara, California 93106
TWX: 910-334-4902
NUC Code: CU-SB

University of California, Santa Cruz
Interlibrary Loan Service
The University Library
Santa Cruz, California 95064
TWX: 910-598-4408
NUC Code: CU-SC

University of the Pacific Library
Interlibrary Loan (for loan), or Service
(for Xerox copy)
Stockton, California 95211
NUC Code: CS to C

University of Redlands
Armacost Library
Redlands, California 92373

University of Santa Clara
Michel Orradre Library
Santa Clara, California 95053

University of Southern California
Library Photoduplication Service
University Park
Los Angeles, California 90007
NUC Code: CLSU

COLORADO

Bureau of Reclamation
Engineering and Research Center
P.O. Box 25007, Denv. Fed. Ctr.
Denver, Colorado 80225
Telex: 4-5737

Colorado College
Interlibrary Loan
Tutt Library
Colorado Springs, Colorado 80903
NUC Code: CoC

Colorado School of Mines
Arthur Lakes Library
Golden, Colorado 80401
NUC Code: CoG

Colorado State University Libraries
Interlibrary Loan Department
Fort Collins, Colorado 80523
TWX: 910-930-9008
NUC Code: CoFS

The Iliff School of Theology
Ira J. Taylor Library
2233 So. University Blvd.
Denver, Colorado 80210
NUC Code: CoDI

University of Colorado Libraries
Interlibrary Loan Service
Boulder, Colorado 80309
TWX: 910-940-5892
NUC Code: CoU

University of Denver
Interlibrary Loan
University of Denver Libraries
Denver, Colorado 80208
TWX: 910-931-2532
NUC Code: CoDU

University of Northern Colorado
Michener Library
Greeley, Colorado 80639
TWX: 910-922-5925
NUC Code: CoGrU

USAF Academy Library
Interlibrary Loan (ILL)
USAF Academy, Colorado 80840

CONNECTICUT

The Connecticut Historical Society
Photographic Reproductions
1, Elizabeth Street
Hartford, Connecticut 06105

Trinity College
Trinity College Library
Hartford, Connecticut 06106
NUC Code: CtHT

University of Connecticut Library
Interlibrary Loan Department
University of Connecticut
Storrs, Connecticut 06268
TWX: 710-420-0571
NUC Code: CtU

University of Hartford
Mortensen Library
200 Bloomfield Avenue
West Hartford, Connecticut 06117
NUC Code: CtWeHAR

Wesleyan University Library
Interlibrary Loans
Middletown, Connecticut 06457
NUC Code: CtW

Yale University Library
Interlibrary Loans
Box 1603A Yale Station
New Haven, Connecticut 06520
NUC Code: CtY

Yale University Divinity Library
409 Prospect St.
New Haven, Connecticut 06510
NUC Code: CtY-D

Yale University
Yale Medical Library
% Interlibrary Loan
333 Cedar Street
New Haven, Connecticut 06510
TWX: 710-465-1145
NUC Code: CtY-M

DELAWARE

The Historical Society of Delaware
505 Market Street
Wilmington, Delaware 19801

University of Delaware
University Library
Interlibrary Loan
Newark, Delaware 19711
TWX: 510-666-0850
NUC Code: DeU

DISTRICT OF COLUMBIA

American University Library
Interlibrary Loan Service
Washington, DC 20016
TWX: 710-822-9277
NUC Code: DAU

Catholic University of America
Interlibrary Loan Service
John K. Mullen of Denver Memorial
Library
Washington, DC 20064
TWX: 710-822-9280
NUC Code: DCU

Folger Shakespeare Library
Photoduplication Department
201 East Capital Street, S.E.
Washington, DC 20003
NUC Code: DFo

George Washington University Library
2130 H St., NW
Washington, DC 20052
TWX: 710-822-9278
NUC Code: DGW

Georgetown University
Lavinger Library
Washington, DC 20057
TWX: 710-822-9284

Library of Congress
Photoduplication Service
10 First Street, S.E.
Washington, DC, 20540
TWX: 710-822-0185
NUC Code: DLC

National Archives Library
Room 302
8th St. & Pennsylvania Ave, NW
Washington, DC 20408
NUC Code: DNA

Smithsonian Institution
Office of Printing & Photographic
Services
Services Branch, MHT CB-054
Washington, DC 20560

U.S. Bureau of the Census
Library Branch
Administrative Services Division
FOB No. 3
Washington, DC 20233

U.S. Department of the Interior
Natural Resources Library
18th and C Streets, NW
Washington, DC 20240
NUC Code: DNRL

U.S. Patent and Trademark Office
Scientific Library
Washington, DC 20231

Veterans Administration
Central Office Library (142D1)
810 Vermont Avenue, NW
Washington, DC 20240

FLORIDA

Florida Atlantic University Library
Interlibrary Loan
Boca Raton, Florida 33432
TWX: 510-953-7532
NUC Code: FBrU (old)
FBoU (new)

Florida Institute of Technology
Library
Interlibrary Loans
P.O. Box 1150
Melbourne, Florida 32901

Florida International University
Tamiami Trail
Miami, Florida 33199
TWX: 810-848-8839
OCLC Code: FXG

Florida State University
Interlibrary Loan Office
R.M. Strozier Library
Tallahassee, Florida 32306
TWX: 810-931-3622U
Answerback: FSU LIBRARY
NUC Code: FTaSU
Note: All requests must be submitted
on the standard ALA ILL form.

Florida State University College of
Law
Room 238 B.K. Roberts Hall
Tallahassee, Florida 32306
NUC Code: FTASU-L

Florida Technological University
Library
Attention: Interlibrary Loan
P.O. Box 25000
Orlando, Florida 32816
TWX: 810-850-0102
NUC Code: FOT

State Library of Florida
Interlibrary Loan
R.A. Gray Building
Tallahassee, Florida 32303
TWX: 810-931-3689
NUC Code: F; OCLO - FBA

University of Florida Libraries
Gainesville, Florida 32611

University of Miami
Interlibrary Loan
Otto G. Richter Library
Coral Gables, Florida 33124
TWX: 810-848-7042
NUC Code: FMU

University of South Florida
The Library
Tampa, Florida 33620
TWX: 810-876-0601
NUC Code: FTS

University of West Florida
Interlibrary Loans
Pensacola, Florida 32504
TWX: 510-737-7957

GEORGIA

Emory University
Interlibrary Loans
The Robert W. Woodruff Library for
Advanced Studies
Atlanta, Georgia 30322
NUC Code: GEU

Georgia Department of Education
Readers Services
Division of Public Library Services
156 Trinity Avenue, SW
Atlanta, Georgia 30303
NUC Code: GAE-P

Georgia Historical Society
501 Whitaker Street
Savannah, Georgia 31401

Georgia Institute of Technology
Price Gilbert Memorial Library
Atlanta, Georgia 30332
TWX: 810-751-8639
NUC Code: GAT

Middle Georgia College
Roberts Memorial Library
Cochran, Georgia 31014

University of Georgia Libraries
Interlibrary Loan
Athens, Georgia 30602
Telex: 810-754-3908
NUC Code: GU

HAWAII

Hawaii State Library
Interloans
478 South King Street
Honolulu, Hawaii 96813
NUC Code: HH

[State of Hawaii]
Office of Library Services
Department of Education
478 S. King Street
Honolulu, Hawaii 96813

Georgia State Library
301 Judicial Building
40 Capitol Square
Atlanta, Georgia 30334

Georgia State University
William R. Pullen Library
Interlibrary Loan Service
104 Decatur Street, SE
Atlanta, Georgia 30303
NUC Code: GASU

Mercer University
Eugene W. Stetson Memorial Library
Macon, Georgia 31207

University of Hawaii
Interlibrary Loan
Hamilton Library
2550 The Mall
Honolulu, Hawaii 96822
Telex: 949-7949
NUC Code: HU

IDAHO

Idaho State Library
325 W. State Street
Boise, Idaho 83702
NUC Code: ID

Idaho State University Library
ILL Department
Pocatello, Idaho 83209
NUC Code: ID PI

University of Idaho Library
Interlibrary Loans
Moscow, Idaho 83843
NUC Code: IdU

ILLINOIS

American Library Association
Headquarters Library
50 East Huron Street
Chicago, Illinois 60611

Center for Research Libraries
Circulation Department
5721 S. Cottage Grove Avenue
Chicago, Illinois 60637
TWX: 910-221-1136
NUC Code: ICRL

Chicago Historical Society Library
Clark St. at North Ave.
Chicago, Illinois 60614

Chicago Municipal Reference Library
Room 1004; 121 N. LaSalle St.
Chicago, Illinois 60602
NUC Code: ICMR

Chicago Public Library
425 N. Michigan Avenue
Chicago, Illinois 60611
TWX: 910-221-1401
NUC Code: IC

Chicago State University
Douglas Library
95th Street & King Drive
Chicago, Illinois 60628

Chicago Theological Seminary
Hammond Library
5757 University Avenue
Chicago, Illinois 60637
NUC Code: ICT

Field Museum of Natural History
Interlibrary Loan
Roosevelt Road at Lake Shore Drive
Chicago, Illinois 60605
NUC Code: ICF

Governors State University
Learning Resources Center
Park Forest South, Illinois 60466
TWX: 910-651-1871
NUC Code: 1 PFSG

Illinois State University
Interlibrary Loan
Milner Library
Normal, Illinois 61761
TWX: 510-352-19-97
NUC Code: INS

Illinois Wesleyan University Library
Interlibrary Loan Department
Bloomington, Illinois 61701
NUC Code: IBLOW

The John Crerar Library
Photoduplication Service
35 W. 33rd Street
Chicago, Illinois 60616
TWX: 910-221-5131
NUC Code: ICJ

Loyola University Library
6525 N. Sheridan Road
Chicago, Illinois 60626
TWX: 910-221-5668
NUC Code: ICL

Newberry Library
60 W. Walton
Chicago, Illinois 60610
NUC Code: ICN

Northeastern Illinois University
Library
5500 North St. Louis Avenue
Chicago, Illinois 60625
OCLC Code: IOA

Northern Illinois University
University Libraries
DeKalb, Illinois 60115
TWX: 910-636-2876
NUC Code: IDeKN

Northwestern University Library
Interlibrary Loan Services
Evanston, Illinois 60201
TWX: 910-231-0872
NUC Code: IEN

Roosevelt University Library
Interlibrary Loans
430 South Michigan Avenue
Chicago, Illinois 60605

Rosary College
Rebecca Crown Library
7900 West Division Street
River Forest, Illinois 60305
NUC Code: IRivfR

Sangamon State University Library
Interlibrary Loans
Springfield, Illinois 62708
TWX: 910-242-0531

Southern Illinois University
Lovejoy Library
Interlibrary Loan
Edwardsville, Illinois 62026
NUC Code: IEdS

Southern Illinois University
Morris Library
Interlibrary Loan Department
Carbondale, Illinois 62901
TWX: 510-520-5773
NUC Code: ICarbS

University of Chicago
The Joseph Regenstein Library
Department of Photocuplication
1100 East 57th Street
Chicago, Illinois 60637

University of Illinois at Chicago
Circle
The Library
Box 8198
Chicago, Illinois 60680
TWX: 910-221-0028
NUC Code: ICIU

University of Illinois at
Urbana-Champaign
The Library
Urbana, Illinois 61801
TWX: 910-245-0780
NUC Code: IU
Requests for reprographic service
and interlibrary loans from Illinois
addresses only should be sent to:
ATTN: R & R Section, Room 128
Library
ILL requests from others (U.S., its
possessions & Canada only) should
be sent to: ATTN: Interlibrary
Lending Division, Room 231
Library
Reprographic service requests from
others (no geographical limit) should,
be sent to: ATTN: Photographic
Services, Room 44 Library

INDIANA

Ft. Wayne Public Library
900 Webster St.
Ft. Wayne, Indiana 46802
TWX: 810-332-1409
NUC Code: InFw

Indiana Historical Society Library
315 West Ohio St.
Indianapolis, Indiana 46202
NUC Code: InHi

Indiana State Library
Reference & Loan Division
140 N. Senate Avenue
Indianapolis, Indiana 46204
TWX: 810-341-3134
NUC Code: In

Indiana State University
Cunningham Memorial Library
Interlibrary Loan
Terre Haute, Indiana 74809
TWX: 810-351-1386
NUC Code: InTi

Indiana University Library
Reference Department
Bloomington, Indiana 47401

Lake County Public Library
1919 W. Lincoln Highway
Merrillville, Indiana 46410
TWX: 910-690-4980

Purdue University
Interlibrary Loan Office
Stewart Center—Libraries
West Lafayette, Indiana 47907
TWX: 810-342-1892
NUC Code: InLP

University of Notre Dame
Memorial Library
Notre Dame, Indiana 46556
NUC Code: Innd

IOWA

Iowa State University
Interlibrary Loan
Library
Ames, Iowa 50010
TWX: 910-520-1159
NUC Code: IaAs

State Library Commission of Iowa
Periodical Bank
E. 12th and Grand
Des Moines, Iowa 50319
TWX: 910-520-2665
NUC Code: Ia

University of Iowa Libraries
Interlibrary Loan Services
Iowa City, Iowa 52242
TWX: 910-525-1391
NUC Code: IaU

KANSAS

Emporia State University
Interlibrary Loans
William Allen White Library
Emporia, Kansas 66801
TWX: 910-740-1665
NUC Code: KEmT

Kansas State Library
4th Floor—535 Kansas Avenue
Topeka, Kansas 66610
TWX: 910-744-6728
NUC Code: K

Kansas State Historical Society
120 W. 10th Street
Topeka, Kansas 66612

Kansas State University Library
Interlibrary Loan
Manhattan, Kansas 66506
TWX: 910-749-6528
NUC Code: KMK

Pittsburg State University
Interlibrary Loans
Library
Pittsburg, Kansas 66762
TWX: 910-740-1391
NUC Code: KPT

University of Kansas Libraries
Interlibrary Services
Lawrence, Kansas 66045
TWX: 910-749-6571
NUC Code: KU

Wichita State University Library
Interlibrary Loan
Wichita, Kansas 67208
TWX: 910-741-6972
NUC Code: KWiU

KENTUCKY

Eastern Kentucky University
John Grant Crabbe Library
Richmond, Kentucky 40475

Kentucky Department of Library &
Archives
Reference Department
Box 537, Berry Hill
Frankfort, Kentucky 40601
TWX: 510-543-3581

Kentucky Historical Society
Library
Box H
Frankfort, Kentucky 40601

Louisville Free Public Library
Reference Services
Fourth and York Streets
Louisville, Kentucky 40302
NUC Code: KyLo

University of Kentucky
M. I. King Library
Balknap Campus
Louisville, Kentucky 40208
TWX: 510-476-8816
NUC Code: KyU

University of Louisville Library
Interlibrary Loan
Belknap Campus
Louisville, Kentucky 40208
TWX: 810-535-3036
NUC Code: KyLoU

Western Kentucky University
Helm Cravens Library
Bowling Green, Kentucky 42101
TWX: 810-531-3653

LOUISIANA

Centenary College Library
P.O. Box 4188
Shreveport, Louisiana 71104
NUC Code: LShC

Louisiana State Library
Interlibrary Loan Division
P.O. Box 131
Baton Rouge, Louisiana 70821
TWX: 510-993-3539
NUC Code: L

Louisiana State University
Photoduplications Department or
Interlibrary Loan Department
Baton Rouge, Louisiana 70803
TWX: 510-993-3427
NUC Code: LU

Louisiana Tech University
Prescott Memorial Library
Tech Station
Ruston, Louisiana 71272
TWX: 510-974-4373
NUC Code: LRuL

Loyola University in New Orleans
University Library, Box 198
6363 St. Charles Avenue
New Orleans, Louisiana 70118

McNeese State University
Frazar Memorial Library
Lake Charles, Louisiana 70609
NUC Code: LLcM

New Orleans Public Library
Louisiana Division
219 Loyola Avenue
New Orleans, Louisiana 70140
TWX: 810-951-5320
NUC Code: LN

Northeast Louisiana University
Sandel Library
Monroe, Louisiana 71209
TWX: 510-977-5373
Call Back: LMN-MRO La
NUC Code: LMN

University of Southwestern
Louisiana
Dupre Library
P.O. Box 4-0199
Lafayette, Louisiana 70504
Telex: 510-975-5074
NUC Code: LLafS

Tulane University Library
Photoduplication Department
New Orleans, Louisiana 70118
TWX: 810-951-5390
NUC Code: LNHT

University of New Orleans
Interlibrary Loan Division
Earl K. Long Library
Lake Front
New Orleans, Louisiana 70122
NUC Code: LU-NO

MAINE

Bangor Public Library
145 Harlow Street
Bangor, Maine 04401
TWX: 710-222-6414
NUC Code: MeBa

Maine State Library
Dept. of Educational and Cultural
Services
Cultural Building
Augusta, Maine 04333
TWX: 710-2266-444

University of Maine at Orono
Fogler Library
Interlibrary Loan Department
Orono, Maine 04473
TWX: 710-229-1096
NUC Code: MeU

MARYLAND

Johns Hopkins University
Milton S. Eisenhower Library
Interlibrary Loan Department
34th & Charles Streets
Baltimore, Maryland 21218
TWX: 710-234-1090
NUC Code: MdBJ

Maryland Historical Society
Library
201 West Monument Street
Baltimore, Maryland 21201
Telex: 301-685-3750

Maryland State Library
Courts of Appeal Building
361 Rowe Boulevard
Annapolis, Maryland 21401

National Agricultural Library
Lending Division
Beltsville, Maryland 20705
TWX: 710-828-0506
NUC Code: DNAL

National Library of Medicine
History of Medicine Division
8600 Rockville Pike
Bethesda, Maryland 20014
OR
Loan and Stack Section
Reference Services Division
8600 Rockville Pike
Bethesda, Maryland 20014
TWX: 710-824-9615
NUC Code DNLM

Towson State University
Albert S. Cook Library
Reference Department
Baltimore, Maryland 21204
NUC Code: MBT

University of Maryland
Interlibrary Loan
Mckeldin Library
College Park, Maryland 20742
TWX: 710-826-1128
NUC Code MdU

MASSACHUSETTS

American Antiquarian Society
185 Salisbury Street
Worcester, Massachusetts 01609
NUC Code: MWA

American Jewish Historical Society
2 Thornton Road
Waltham, Massachusetts 02154

Amherst College Library
Interlibrary Loans
Amherst, Massachusetts 01002
NUC Code: MA

Boston Athenaeum
10½ Beacon Street
Boston, Massachusetts 02108
NUC Code: MBAt

Boston College Libraries
Interlibrary Loans
Chestnut Hill, Massachusetts 02167
NUC Code: MChB

Boston Public Library
Interlibrary Loan
Boston, Massachusetts 02117
TWX: 710-321-0513
NUC Code: MB

Boston University
Mugar Memorial Library
771 Commonwealth Avenue
Boston, Massachusetts 02215
NUC Code: MBU

Brandeis University
Interlibrary Loan Service
Goldfarb Library
(Or: Gerstenzang Science Library)
Waltham, Massachusetts 02154
NUC Code: MWalB

Bridgewater State College
The Clement C. Maxwell Library
Reference Department
Bridgewater, Massachusetts 02324

Clark University
Robert Hutchings Goddard Library
Worcester, Massachusetts 01610

Essex Institute
James Duncan Phillips Library
132 Essex Street
Salem, Massachusetts 01970
NUC Code: MSaE

Harvard University
Photographic Division,
Widener Library
Cambridge, Massachusetts 03138
NUC Code: MH

Harvard University
Arnold Arboretum Library
Gray Hervarium Library
22 Divinity Avenue
Cambridge, Massachusetts 02138
NUC Code: MH-A/G

Harvard University
Tozzer Library of the Peabody
Museum
Interlibrary Loans
21 Divinity Avenue
Cambridge, Massachusetts 02138
NUC Code: MH-P

Harvard Business School
Interlibrary Loans
Baker Library
Boston, Massachusetts 02163
NUC Code: MH-BA

Marine Biological Laboratory
Library
Woods Hole, Massachusetts 02543
TWX: 710-346-6601
NUC Code: MWhB

Massachusetts Historical Society
Library
1154 Boylston Street
Boston, Massachusetts 02215
NUC Code: MHi

Massachusetts Institute of
Technology
Microreproduction Laboratory
Room 14-0551
Cambridge, Massachusetts 02139

Mount Holyoke College Library
Interlibrary Loan
South Hadley, Massachusetts 01075
NUC Code: MSM

Museum of Fine Arts
William Morris Hunt Memorial
Library
Interlibrary Loan
Boston, Massachusetts 02115
NUC Code: MBMu

New England Historic Genealogical
Society
101 Newbury Street
Boston, Massachusetts 02116

Northeastern University Library
Interlibrary Loans
360 Huntington Ave.
Boston, Massachusetts 02215
NST Code: MBNU

Simmons College Library
Reference Department—ILL
300 The Fenway
Boston, Massachusetts 02215
NUC Code: MBSi

Smith College Library
Interlibrary Loan Service
Reference Department
Northampton, Massachusetts 01060
NUC Code: MNS

State Library of Massachusetts
Chief of Reference Services
341 State House
Boston, Massachusetts 02133
NUC Code: M

Tufts University Library
Medford, Massachusetts 02155
NUC Code: MMet

University of Massachusetts
Library
Interlibrary Loan
Amherst, Massachusetts 01003
NUC Code: MU

University of Massachusetts—Boston
Interlibrary Loan
Boston, Massachusetts 02215
NUC Code: MBMU (not MBMU—the
Museum of Fine Arts code)

Wellesley College Library
Interlibrary Loan Service
Wellesley, Massachusetts 02181
NUC Code: MWelC

Williams College Library
Williamstown, Massachusetts 01267
NUC Code: MWiW

MICHIGAN

Andrews University
Interlibrary Loan Service
James White Library
Berrien Springs, Michigan 49104
NUC Code: MiBsA

Detroit Public Library
Interlibrary Loan
5201 Woodward Avenue
Detroit, Michigan 48202
NUC Code: MiD

Eastern Michigan University
Interlibrary Loan—C.E.R. 315
Ypsilanti, Michigan 48197
NUC Code: MiYEM

Michigan State University Libraries
Interlibrary Lending Service
East Lansing, Michigan 48824
TWX: 810-251-0875
NUC Code: MiEM

Michigan Technological University
Library
Interlibrary Loan
Houghton, Michigan 49931
NUC Code: MiHM

Northern Michigan University
Library
Marquette, Michigan 49855

Raisin Valley Library System
3700 South Custer Road
Monroe, Michigan 48161

State Library—Michigan
Interlibrary Loan Office
P.O. Box 30007
Lansing, Michigan 48909

University Microfilms International
300 N. Zeeb Road
Ann Arbor, Michigan 48106
Toll-free No.: 800-521-0600

University of Detroit Main Library
Interlibrary Loans
4001 West McNichols
Detroit, Michigan 48221
NUC Code: MiDU

University of Michigan
Interlibrary Loan
Hatcher Graduate Library
Ann Arbor, Michigan 48109
TWX: 810-223-6016
NUC Code: MiU

Wayne State University
Interlibrary Loan Department
Purdy Library
Detroit, Michigan 48202
TWX (Medical Library):
810-221-5163

MINNESOTA

Carleton College Library
Interlibrary Services
Northfield, Minnesota 55057
TWX: 910-565-2182
NUC Code: MnNC
OCLC Code: MNN

James J. Hill Reference Library
Photoduplication Services
80 West Fourth St.
St. Paul, Minnesota 55102
TWX: 910-563-3557
NUC Code: MNSJA

Minneapolis Public Library &
Information Center
300 Nicollet Mall
Minneapolis, Minnesota 55401
TWX: 910-576-2784
NUC Code: MnM

Minnesota Department of Education
Office of Public Libraries
And Interlibrary Cooperation
301 Cedar Street
St. Paul, Minnesota 55101
TWX: 910-563-3571

Minnesota Historical Society Library
690 Cedar Street
St. Paul, Minnesota 55101
NUC Code: MnHi

Office of Public Libraries, MN Dept. of
Educ., SEE Minnesota Dept. of Educ.
Office of Public Libraries
TWX: 910-563-3511

University of Minnesota
Interlibrary Loans Division
179 Wilson Library
Minneapolis, Minnesota 55455
TWX: 910-576-3491
NUC Code: MnU

University of Minnesota—Morris
The Rodney A. Briggs Library
Morris, Minnesota 56267
NUC Code: MnMoU

University of Minnesota Technical
College, Waseca
Learning Resources Center
Waseca, Minnesota 56093
TWX: 910-565-2163
OCLC Code: MnWaSU

University of Minnesota
Twin Cities Campus Libraries
Interlibrary Loans
St. Paul Campus Library
St. Paul, Minnesota 55108
TWX: 910-576-3491 (limited access,
requests received by TWX in Wilson
Library, Mpls. Campus will be
processes and forwarded to St. Paul
Campus Library
NUC Code: MnU-A

MISSISSIPPI

Mississippi State University
Interlibrary Loan Department
Mitchell Memorial Library
P.O. Box 5408
Mississippi State, Mississippi 39762
TWX: 510-983-3063 (Library also
has Telecopier Service:
601-323-6035
NUC Code: MssM

University of Mississippi Library
Interlibrary Loans
University, Mississippi 38677
TWX: 510-980-2058
NUC Code: MsU

University of Southern Mississippi
Cook Library
Interlibrary Loan Department
Box 53, Southern Station
Hattiesburg, Mississippi 39401
NUC Code: MsHaU

MISSOURI

Concordia Seminary Library
801 De Mun Avenue
St. Louis, Missouri 63105
NUC Code: MosCs

Drury College
Walker Library
Springfield, Missouri 65802
NUC Code: MoSpD

Harry S. Truman Library
24 Highway at Delaware
Independence, Missouri 64050

Linda Hall Library
Interlibrary Loan
5109 Cherry Street
Kansas City, Missouri 64110
NUC Code: MoKL

Missouri State Library
Interlibrary Loan
308 E. High St.
Jefferson City, Missouri 65101
TWX: 910-760-2454
NUC Code: Mo

Northeast Missouri State University
Pickler Memorial Library
Kirksville, Missouri 63501
NUC Code: MoKiU

Northwest Missouri State University
Wells Library
Interlibrary Loans
Maryville, Missouri 64468

Seminex (Concordia Seminary in
Exile)
607 North Grand Boulevard
St. Louis, Missouri 63103
NUC Code: MoSCSEx

State Historical Society of Missouri
Hitt and Lowry Streets
Columbia, Missouri 65201

University of Missouri Library
Interlibrary Lending Service
Circulation Department
Columbia, Missouri 65201
TWX: 910-760-1451
NUC Code: MoU

University of Missouri—Kansas City
Interlibrary Loans, General Library
5100 Rockhill Rd.
Kansas City, Missouri 64110
NUC Code: MoKU

University of Missouri—Rolla
Library
Rolla, Missouri 65401
NUC Code: MoRM

University of Missouri—St. Louis
Interlibrary Loans
8001 Natural Bridge Road
St. Louis, Missouri 63121
NUC Code: MoU-St

Washington University Libraries
ILL Division, John M. Olin Library
St. Louis, Missouri 63130
TWX: 910-761-0452
NUC Code: MoSW

MONTANA

Great Falls Public Library
2nd Ave. N. & 3rd St.
Great Falls, Montana 59401
TWX: 910-975-1945

Montana Historical Society, Library
225 No. Roberts
Helena, Montana 59601
NUC Code: MHS

Montana State University Library
Interlibrary Loans
Bozeman, Montana 59717
TWX: 910-963-2062
NUC Code: MtBC

University of Montana Library
Interlibrary Loans
Missoula, Montana 59812
TWX: 910-963-2048
NUC Code: MtU

NEBRASKA

Nebraska State Historical Society
1500 "R" Street
Lincoln, Nebraska 68508

Nebraska Wesleyan University
Cochrane-Woods Library
Lincoln, Nebraska 68504

University of Nebraska-Lincoln
Interlibrary Loan Service
Love Memorial Library
Lincoln, Nebraska 68588
TWX: 910-621-8232
NUC Code: NbU

NEVADA

Nevada Historical Society
1650 North Virginia Street
Reno, Nevada 89503

Nevada State Library
Public Services Division
Capitol Complex
Carson City, Nevada 89710
TWX: 910-359-0139
NUC Code: Nv

University of Nevada Library
Interlibrary Loan Department
Reno, Nevada 89557
TWX: 910-395-7054
Answerback: NVU LIB RENO
NUC Code: NvU

NEW HAMPSHIRE

Dartmouth College
Interlibrary Loan Service
Baker Library
Hanover, New Hampshire 03755
TWX: 710-366-1829
NUC Code: NhD

New Hampshire Historical Society
30 Park Street
Concord, New Hampshire 03301
Telex: 603-225-3381
NUC Code: NhHi

New Hampshire State Library
20 Park St.
Concord, New Hampshire 03301
TWX: 710-361-6467
NUC Code: Nh

University of New Hampshire
Interlibrary Loans—Library
Durham, New Hampshire 03824
TWX: 510-297-4441
NUC Code: NhU

NEW JERSEY

Cherry Hill Free Public Library
1100 Kings Highway North
Cherry Hill, New Jersey 08034

Drew University
Rose Memorial Library
Madison, New Jersey 07940
NUC Code: Njmd

Fairleigh Dickinson University
Library
Madison, New Jersey 07940

New Jersey State Library
Lending Services
185 W. State Street
Trenton, New Jersey 08625
NUC Code: Nj

Princeton Theological Seminary
Speer Library
Box 111
Princeton, New Jersey 08540
NUC Code: NjPT

Princeton University Library
Photographic Services
Princeton, New Jersey 08540
NUC Code: NjP

Rutgers University
Interlibrary Loan
Alexander Library
New Brunswick, New Jersey 08903
(For material in social sciences,
humanities & education)
AND
Interlibrary Loans
Library of Science and Medicine
New Brunswick, New Jersey 08903
(For material in science, technology,
engineering, medicine and
psychology)

Rutgers University
Library of Science and Medicine
P.O. Box 1029
Piscataway, New Jersey 08854
NUC Code: NjR

NEW MEXICO

New Mexico State University
Library
Interlibrary Loan
Box 3475
Las Cruces, New Mexico
TWX: 910-983-0555
NUC Code: NmLcU

University of Albuquerque Library
St. Joseph's Pl. NW
Albuquerque, New Mexico 87140

University of New Mexico
General Library
Interlibrary Loan Office
Albuquerque, New Mexico 87131
TWX: 910-989-1641
NUC Code: NmU

NEW YORK

Alfred University
Herrick Memorial Library
Alfred, New York 14802
NUC Code: NALF

Brooklyn Museum
Art Reference Library
Brooklyn, New York 11238
NUC Code: NBB

The Brooklyn Museum
Wilbour Library of Egyptology
Eastern Parkway
Brooklyn, New York 11238

Brooklyn Public Library
Grand Army Plaza
Brooklyn, New York 11238
TWX: 488-3529

Calspan Corporation
Technical Library
P.O. Box 235
Buffalo, New York 14221
NUC Code: NBuCa

City University of New York
Graduate Center Library
Interlibrary Loans
33 West 42nd Street
New York, New York 10036
TWX: 710-581-5254
NUC Code: NNCU-G

Clarkson College of Tech.
Library
Potsdam, New York 13676 ·
TWX: 510-259-5162
NUC Code: NPoTC

Colgate University Library
Reference Department
Hamilton, New York 13346
NUC Code: NHC

Columbia University Libraries
Reprographic Services
Box 17, Butler Library
New York, New York 10027
NUC Code: NNC

Columbia University
Teachers College Library
525 West 120 Street
New York, New York 10027
TWX: 710-581-4433
NUC Code: NNC-T

Cornell University Libraries
Interlibrary Lending & Cooperative
Reference Services
Ithaca, New York 14853
TWX: 510-255-9301
NUC Code: NIC

Engineering Societies Library
345 East 47th Street
New York, New York 10017
NUC Code: NNE

Fordham University Library
Reference Department
Bronx, New York 10458
NUC Code: NNF

The Foundation Center
888 Seventh Avenue
New York, New York 10019

General Theological Seminary
St. Mark's Library
175 Ninth Avenue
New York, New York 10011
NUC Code: NNG

Hispanic Society of America Library
Curator of Rare Books and
Manuscripts
613 West 155th Street
New York, New York 10032

The Metropolitan Museum of Art
The Thomas J. Watson Library
Fifth Avenue at 82nd Street
New York, New York 10028
NUC Code: NNMM

New York Academy of Medicine
Library
2 East 103rd Street
New York, New York 10029
TWX: 710-581-6131
NUC Code: NNNAM

The New York Botanical Garden
The Library
Bronx, New York 10458
NUC Code: NNBG

New York City Community College
Library
300 Jay Street
Brooklyn, New York 11201
NUC Code: NBNC

The New York Public Library
Photographic Service
Fifth Avenue at 42nd Street
New York, New York 10018

New York State Library
Interlibrary Loan Section
Cultural Education Center
Empire State Plaza
Albany, New York 12223
Data Phone: 518-474-5786
TWX: 710-441-8770
NUC Code: N

New York State Historical
Association
Cooperstown, New York 13326

New York University
E. H. Bobst Library
70 Washington Square South
New York, New York 10012
NUC Code: NNU

Polytechnic Institute of New York
Library
333 Jay Street
Brooklyn, New York 11201
NUC Code: NBPOL

Pratt Institute Library
215 Ryerson Street
Brooklyn, New York 11205

Rensselaer Polytechnic Institute
Interlibrary Loan Office
Folsom Library
Troy, New York 12181
NUC Code: NTR

St. John's University Library
Interlibrary Loan
Grand Central & Utopia Parkways
Jamaica, New York 11439
NUC Code: NNStJ

State University College
Interlibrary Loan
James M. Milne Library
Oneonta, New York 13820
NUC Code: NOneoU

State University College/Oswego
Penfield Library—Interlibrary Loan
Dept.
Oswego, New York 13126
TWX: 710-547-0659
NUC Code: NOsU

State University College at
Plattsburgh
Benjamin F. Feinberg Library
Interlibrary Loan
Plattsburgh, New York 12901
TWX: 510-251-6706

State University of New York at
Albany
Interlibrary Loans, Room 110
University Library
1400 Washington Avenue
Albany, New York 12222
TWX: 710-441-8257
NUC Code: NAIU

State University of New York at
Buffalo
Lockwood Memorial Library
Buffalo, New York 14214

State University of New York at
Stony Brook
University Libraries
Reference Department
Interlibrary Loans
Stony Brook, New York 11794
TWX: 510-228-7760
NUC Code: NSbSU

Syracuse University
Interlibrary Lending Service
116 E. S. Bird Library
Syracuse, New York 13210
TWX: 710-541-0411
NUC Code: NSyU

United Nations
(See United Nations by country)

U.S. Military Academy
USMA Library
West Point, New York 10996

University of Rochester Library
Interlibrary Loans & Photocopy
Section
Rochester, New York 14627
TWX: 510-253-3926
NUC Code: NRU

Vassar College Library
Interlibrary Loan Service
Poughkeepsie, New York 12601
NUC Code: NPV

YIVO Institute for Jewish Research
1048 Fifth Avenue
New York, New York 10033

NORTH CAROLINA

Duke University Library
Interlibrary Loans
Durham, North Carolina 27706
NUC Code: NcD

East Carolina University
Interlibrary Loan
Joyner Library
Greenville, North Carolina 27834
NUC Code: NcGrE

The Historical Foundation of the
Presbyterian and Reformed
Churches
Box 847
Montreat, North Carolina 28757
NUC Code: NCMHI

North Carolina Central University
Interlibrary Loans Librarian
James E. Shepard Memorial Library
Durham, North Carolina 27707

North Carolina Department of
Cultural Resources
Division of State Library
Raleigh, North Carolina 27611

North Carolina State University
Interlibrary Center
D. H. Hill Library
P. O. Box 5007
Raleigh, North Carolina 27607
TWX: 510-928-1847
NUC Code NcRS

University of North Carolina at
Asheville
D. Hiden Ramsey Library
Asheville, North Carolina 28804

University of North Carolina Library
Interlibrary Services Center
G-38 Wilson Library 024-A
Chapel Hill, North Carolina 27514
TWX: 510-920-0760
NUC Code: NcU

University of North Carolina at
Charlotte
Reference Unit—ILL
Charlotte, North Carolina 28223
NUC Code: NcCU

University of North Carolina at
Greensboro
Interlibrary Loans
Jackson Library
Greensboro, North Carolina 27412
NUC Code: NcGU

University of North Carolina at
Wilmington
Interlibrary Loan
William M. Randall Library
Wilmington, North Carolina 28401
NUC Code: NcWU

Wake Forest University, Bowman
Grey School of Medicine Library
Winston-Salem, North Carolina
27103
TWX: 510-931-3386

Western.Carolina University
Hunter Library
Cullowhee, North Carolina 28723
NUC Code: NcCuW

NORTH DAKOTA

North Dakota State Library
Highway 83 North
Bismark, North Dakota 58505
TWX: 910-677-234
NUC Code: NdLibC

North Dakota State University
Library
Interlibrary Loan
Fargo, North Dakota 58102
TWX: 910-673-8320
NUC Code: NdFa

University of North Dakota
Chester Fritz Library
Interlibrary Loan Office
Grand Forks, North Dakota 58202
TWX: 910-673-8394
(NdUGFGRFO)
NUC Code: NdU

OHIO

Antioch College
Interlibrary Loan
Olive Kettering Library
Yellow Springs, Ohio 45387
NUC Code: OYesA

Bowling Green State University
Library
Interlibrary Loan Service
Bowling Green, Ohio 43403
TWX: 810-499-2989
NUC Code: OBgU

Capital University
Library
Columbus, Ohio 43209

Case Western Reserve University
Interlibrary Loan
Freiberger Library
11161 E. Boulevard
Cleveland, Ohio 44106
TWX: 810-421-8818
NUC Code: OCIW

Case Western Reserve University
Sears Library
Interlibrary Service
10900 Euclid Avenue
Cleveland, Ohio 44106
TWX: 810-421-8818
NUC Code: OCLCS pre-1969 included
with Freiberger Library, after 1969 in
OCIW

The Cincinnati Historical Society
Eden Park
Cincinnati, Ohio 45202

Cleveland Public Library
Photoduplication Office
325 Superior Avenue
Cleveland, Ohio 44114
NUC Code: OCl

College of Wooster
Andrews Library
Photoduplication Service
Wooster, Ohio 44691
NUC Code: OWoC

Public Library of Columbus and
Franklin County
General Reference Division
28 South Hamilton Road
Columbus, Ohio 43213
TWX: 810-482-1161
NUC Code: OCO

Denison University
W. H. Doane Library
Granville, Ohio 43023
NUC Code: OgraD

Hebrew Union College Library
Photoduplication Department
3101 Clifton Avenue
Cincinnati, Ohio 45220
NUC Code: OCH

Kent State University
University Libraries
Kent, Ohio 44242
TWX: 810-431-2335
NUC Code: OKENTU

Malone College
Everett L. Cattell Library
515 25th St. N.W.
Canton, Ohio 44709

Miami University Libraries
Interlibrary Loan
Oxford, Ohio 45056
TWX: 810-470-8486
NUC Code: OOxM

Oberlin College Library
Seeley G. Mudd Learning Center
Interlibrary Loan Service
Oberlin, Ohio 44074
NUC Code: OO

Ohio Northern University
Interlibrary Loans
Heterick Memorial Library
Ada, Ohio 45810
NUC Code: OadN

Ohio State University Libraries
Interlibrary Loan
1858 Neil Avenue
Columbus, Ohio 43210
TWX: 810-482-1042
NUC Code: OU

Ohio University Library
Interlibrary Loan Department
Athens, Ohio 45701
NUC Code: OAU

The Public Library of Cincinnati and
Hamilton County
Interlibrary Loan
800 Vine Street
Cincinnati, Ohio 45202
TWX: 810-461-2300
NUC Code: OC

The Rutherford B. Hayes Library
1337 Hayes Avenue
Fremont, Ohio 43420
NUC Code: OFH

The University of Akron
Bierce Library
Akron, Ohio 44325
TWX: 810-431-2042
NUC Code: OAKU
OCLC Code: AKR

University of Cincinnati Library
Interlibrary   Loan/Duplication
Services
Cincinnati, Ohio 45221
TWX: 810-461-2309
NUC Code: OCU

University of Toledo
Photocopy Service
Carlson Library
Toledo, Ohio 43606
NUC Code: OTU

The Western Reserve
Historical Society
The Library
10825 East Boulevard
Cleveland, Ohio 44106

Wright State University
Interlibrary Loan
University Library
Dayton, Ohio 45431
TWX: 810-475-2999
NUC Code: ODaWU

Youngstown State University
Interlibrary Loan Department
William F. Maag Library
410 Wick Avenue
Youngstown, Ohio 44555
TWX: 810-435-2904
NUC Code: OYC

OKLAHOMA

Northeastern Oklahoma State
University
John Vaughan Library
Learning Resources Center
Tahlequah, Oklahoma 74464

Oklahoma Department of Libraries
Interlibrary Loan
200 N.E. 18th Street
Oklahoma City, Oklahoma 73105
TWX: 910-831-3178
NUC Code: Ok

Oklahoma State University Library
Interlibrary Loan
Stillwater, Oklahoma 74074
TWX: 910-831-3178
(Via OK Dept of Libs)
NUC Code: OkS

University of Oklahoma Libraries
Interlibrary Loan
401 West Brooks, Room 146
Norman, Oklahoma 73019
TWX: 910-831-3178
NUC Code: OkU

The University of Oklahoma
Health Sciences Center Library
P.O. Box 26901
Oklahoma City, Oklahoma 73190
TWX: 910-831-3179
NUC Code: OKU-M

OREGON

Multnomah Law Library
County Courthouse, 4th Floor
Portland, Oregon 97204

Oregon Historical Society, Library
1230 S.W. Park Avenue
Portland, Oregon 97205

Oregon State Library
Interlibrary Loan
Salem, Oregon 97310
TWX: 510-599-0119

Portland State University, Library
934 S. W. Harrison
P.O. Box 1151
Portland, Oregon 97207
TWX: 910-464-1593
NUC Code: OrPS

Reed College
Interlibrary Loans
Portland, Oregon 97202
TWX: 910-464-1591
NUC Code: OrPR

University of Oregon
Interlibrary Loan
Eugene, Oregon 97477
TWX: 510-597-0354
NUC Code: OrU

University of Health Sciences Library
Interlibrary Loans
P.O. Box 573
Portland, Oregon 97207
TWX: 910-464-8063
NUC Code: ORU-M

PENNSYLVANIA

Academy of Natural Sciences of
Philadelphia
Interlibrary Loans
Library
19th Street & The Parkway
Philadelphia, Pennsylvania 19103
NUC Code: PPAN

Allentown College
Library
Center Valley, Pennsylvania 18034
TWX: 510-651-1284
NUC Code: PcVA

American Philosophical Society
Library
105 South Fifth Street
Philadelphia, Pennsylvania 19106

The Balch Institute
18 South Seventh Street
Philadelphia, Pennsylvania 19106
Tel: 215-574-8000

Bryn Mawr College Library
Interlibrary Loans
Bryn Mawr, Pennsylvania 19010
NUC Code: PBm

Bucknell University
Ellen Clarke Bertrand Library
Lewisburg, Pennsylvania 17837
TWX: 510-655-0505
NUC Code: PLeB

Carnegie Library of Pittsburgh
Photocopy Department
4400 Forbes Avenue
Pittsburgh, Pennsylvania 15213
TWX: 710-664-4280

Carnegie-Mellon University
Mellon Institute Library
4400 Fifth Avenue
Pittsburgh, Pennsylvania 15213
NUC Code: PPiM

Carnegie-Mellon University Libraries
Schenley Park
Pittsburgh, Pennsylvania 15213
NUC Code: PPiC

Cedar Crest College Library
Interlibrary Loan
Allentown, Pennsylvania 18104
TWX: 510-651-1309

The College of Physicians of
Philadelphia
Library
19 South 22nd Street
Philadelphia, Pennsylvania 19103
NUC Code: PPC

Drexel University Libraries
Interlibrary Loan Office
32nd & Chestnut Streets
Philadelphia, Pennsylvania 19104
NUC Code: PPD

Duquesne University
Interlibrary Loan Department
Pittsburgh, Pennsylvania 15219
NUC Code: PPiD

The Franklin Institute Library
Photoduplication Unit
20th & The Parkway
Philadelphia, Pennsylvania 19103
NUC Code: PPF

Free Library of Philadelphia
Central Public Services Division
Logan Square
Philadelphia, Pennsylvania 19103

Haverford College
James P. Magill Library
Haverford, Pennsylvania 19041
NUC Code: PHC

Historical Society of Pennsylvania
1300 Locust Street
Philadelphia, Pennsylvania 19107
NUC Code: Phi

Indiana University of Pennsylvania
Rhodes R. Stabley Library
Interlibrary Loan Services
Indiana, Pennsylvania 15701
TWX: 510-468-5275
NUC Code: PInU

Institute for Scientific Information
Oats Department
325 Chestnut Street
Philadelphia, Pennsylvania 19106
Telex: 84-5305

Lafayette College
Interlibrary Loan
David Bishop Skillman Library
Easton, Pennsylvania 18042
TWX: 510-651-2511
NUC Code: PEL

Lehigh University
Interlibrary Loan
Linderman Library No. 30
Bethlehem, Pennsylvania 18015
TWX: 510-651-4740
NUC Code: PBL

The Library Company of
Philadelphia
1314 Locust Street
Philadelphia, Pennsylvania 19107

Muhlenberg College Library
Interlibrary Loan
Allentown, Pennsylvania 18104
TWX: 510-651-1242
NUC Code: PAtM

Osterhout Free Library
Interlibrary Loan
71 S. Franklin Street
Wilkes-Barre, Pennsylvania 18701
NUC Code: PWb

Pennsylvania State University
Photoduplication Services
Pattee Library
University Park, Pennsylvania 16802
TWX: 510-670-3520
NUC Code: PSt

Philadelphia College of Art
Library
Broad and Spruce Streets
Philadelphia, Pennsylvania 19102

Philadelphia College of Textiles &
Sciences
Interlibrary Loan
Pastore Library
School House Lane
Philadelphia, Pennsylvania 19144
NUC Code: PPPTe

State Library of Pennsylvania
General Library Bureau
Box 1601
Harrisburg, Pennsylvania 17126
TWX: 510-650-4923
NUC Code: P

Swarthmore College
Library
Swarthmore, Pennsylvania 19081
NUC Code: PSC

Temple University
Interlibrary Loan Service
Paley Library
Philadelphia, Pennsylvania 19122
TWX: 710-670-1773
NUC Code: PPT

Thomas Jefferson University
Scott Memorial Library
Philadelphia, Pennsylvania 19107
TWX: 710-670-0275

University of Pennsylvania
Library / CH
Interlibrary Loan
3420 Walnut Street
Philadelphia, Pennsylvania 19104
TWX: 710-670-0638
NUC Code: PU

University of Pittsburgh
Hillman Library
Interlibrary Loan Service
Pittsburgh, Pennsylvania 15260
TWX: 710-664-4263
NUC Code: PPiU

Willson College
Interlibrary Loan
John Stewart Memorial Library
Chambersburg, Pennsylvania 17201
TWX: 510-650-4962
NUC Code: PChW

RHODE ISLAND

Brown University Library
Humanities and Social Sciences
John D. Rockefeller Library
Interlibrary Loans
Box A, Brown University
Providence, Rhode Island 02912
AND
Natural Sciences
Sciences Library
Interlibrary Loans
Box I, Brown University
Providence, Rhode Island 02912
NUC Code: RPB

Rhode Island College
Interlibrary Loan
James P. Adams Library
600 Mt. Pleasant Avenue
Providence, Rhode Island 02908
NUC Code: RPRC

Rhode Island Historical Society
Library
121 Hope Street
Providence, Rhode Island 02906

SOUTH CAROLINA

Clemson University
Reference, Cooper Library
Clemson, South Carolina 29631
NUC Code: ScCleU

South Carolina State Library
Interlibrary Loan Service
P.O. Box 11469
Columbia, South Carolina 29211
TWX: 810-666-2148
NUC Code: Sc

University of South Carolina
Thomas Cooper Library
Reference Department
Columbia, South Carolina 29208
TWX: 810-666-2118
NUC Code: ScU

Winthrop College
Reference Department
Dacus Library
Rock Hill, South Carolina 29733
Telex: 57-0349 (Winthrop Roll)
NUC Code: ScRhW

SOUTH DAKOTA

South Dakota State Library
State Library Building
Pierre, South Dakota 57501
TWX: 910-668-2222
NUC Code: Sd

South Dakota State University
Library
Interlibrary Loans
Brookings, South Dakota 57006
TWX: 910-668-6894
NUC Code: SdB

University of South Dakota
I.D. Weeks Library
Vermillion, South Dakota 57069
NUC Code: SdU

TENNESSEE

George Peabody College for
Teachers
Reference Department
Education Library
Box 325
Nashville, Tennessee 37203

Joint University Libraries
Interlibrary Loan
Nashville, Tennessee 37203
NUC Code: TNJ

Memphis/Shelby Co. Public Library
and Information Center
Area Resource Center
1850 Peabody
Memphis, Tennessee 38104
TWX: 810-591-1347
NUC Code: TM

Memphis State University
John Brister Library
Interlibrary Loan
Memphis, Tennessee 38152
TWX: 810-591-1564
NUC Code: TMM

Middle Tennessee State University
Library
Reference Department
Murfreesboro, Tennessee 37132

Tennessee State Library & Archives
Restoration & Reproduction Section
403 7th Avenue North
Nashville, Tennessee 37219

Tennessee Technological University
Reference Department
Jere Whitson Memorial Library
Cookeville, Tennessee 38501
SOLINET: TTU

Tennessee Valley Authority
Technical Library
400 Commerce Avenue E2 A1
Knoxville, Tennessee 37902

University of Tennessee—Knoxville
Interlibrary Services
Library
Knoxville, Tennessee 37916
TWX: 810-583-0176
NUC Code: TU

University of Tennessee at Martin
Paul Meek Library
Interlibrary Loans
Martin, Tennessee 38238
NUC Code: TMaU
OCLC: THM

Venderbilt University
Medical Center Library
Nashville, Tennessee 37232
NUC Code: TNJ-M

TEXAS

Baylor University
Moody Memorial Library
Box 6307
Waco, Texas 76706
TWX: 910-894-5200
NUC Code: TxWB

Dallas Public Library
1954 Commerce Street
Dallas, Texas 75201
TWX: 910-861-4057

East Texas State University
Commerce, Texas 75428
TWX: 910-860-5112

Houston Public Library
Interlibrary Loan
500 McKinney Avenue
Houston, Texas 77002
TWX: 910-881-6227

Lamar University
Mary & John Gray Library
P.O. Box 10021
Lamar University Station
Beaumont, Texas 77710
TWX: 910-884-5137
NUC Code: TxBeal

Lyndon Baines Johnson Library
2313 Red River
Austin, Texas 78705

North   Texas   State   University
Library
Interlibrary Loans—Lending
Denton, Texas 76203
TWX: 510-877-7533
NUC Code: TxDN

Rice University Library
Interlibrary Loan—Lending
Houston, Texas 77001
TWX: 910-881-3766
NUC Code: txHR

Southern Methodist University
Fondren Library
Interlibrary Loan Department
Dallas, Texas 75275
TWX: 910-861-4958
NUC Code: TxDaM

Southwestern Baptist Seminary
Fleming Library
Box 22000-2E
Fort Worth, Texas 76122
NUC Code TxFs

Southwestern University
Cody Memorial Library
Georgetown, Texas 78626
NUC Code: TxGeoS

Texas A&M University Library
Interlibrary Services
College Station, Texas 77843
TWX: 510-892-7945
NUC Code: TXCM

Texas Christian University
Interlibrary Loan Service
Fort Worth, Texas 76129
TWX: 910-893-4065
NUC Code: TxFTC

Texas State Library
Public Services Department
P.O. Box 12927
Capitol Station
Austin, Texas 78711
TWX: 910-874-1367
NUC Code: Tx

Texas Tech University
Library
Interlibrary Loan
Lubbock, Texas 79409
TWX: 910-896-4313
NUC Code: TxLT

Texas Woman's University
Library
Box 23715 TWU Station
Denton, Texas 76204
TWX: 510-877-4597
NUC Code: TxDW

University of Houston Libraries
Interlibrary Loans
Calhoun Rd.
Houston, Texas 77004
TWX: 910-881-3754
NUC Code: TxHU

The University of Texas Health
Science Center
Library at Dallas
5323 Harry Hines Boulevard
Dallas, Texas 75235
TWX: 910-861-4946

University of Texas Medical Branch
Moody Medical Library
Galveston, Texas 77550
Telex: 910-885-5225

The University of Texas at Arlington
Interlibrary Loan
Library
Arlington, Texas 76019

University of Texas at Austin
The General Libraries
Austin, Texas 78712
TWX: 910-874-1304
NUC Code: TxU

The University of Texas at El Paso
Library
El Paso, Texas 79968
TWX: 910-964-1367
ULS & NST Code: TxEM or TxETW

University of Texas at San Antonio
Interlibrary Loan Service
San Antonio, Texas 78285
TWX: 910-871-1247
NUC Code: TxSaU

West Texas State University
Cornette Library
Interlibrary Loan
Box 748, W.F. Station
Canyon, Texas 79016
TWX: 910-899-4291
NUC Code: TxCaW

UTAH

Brigham Young University
Harold B. Lee Library
Provo, Utah 84601
TWX: 910-971-5896

The Church of Jesus Christ of
Latter-Day Saints
Genealogical Department Library
50 East North Temple Street
Salt Lake City, Utah 84150

University of Utah
Libraries
Interlibrary Loans
Salt Lake City, Utah 84112
TWX: 910-925-5172
NUC Code: UU

VERMONT

Vermont Historical Society Library
Pavilion Bldg.
109 State Street
Montpelier, Vermont 05602

University of Vermont
Interlibrary Loan Service
Guy W. Bailey Library
Burlington, Vermont 05401
TWX: 512-299-0023
NUC Code: VtU

VIRGINIA

George Mason University
Fenwick Library
4400 University Drive
Fairfax, Virginia 22030
TWX: 710-833-1177

Old Dominion University
Interlibrary Loans
University Library
Norfolk, Virginia 23508
TWX: 710-881-1120
NUC Code: ViNO

Portsmouth Public Library
601 Court Street
Portsmouth, Virginia 23704

TRW Systems Group
Technical Library
7600 Colshire Drive
McLean, Virginia 22101
TWX: 710-831-0030
FAX: 703-893-7308

Virginia Commonwealth University
James Branch Cabell Library
Interlibrary Loan Department
901 Park Avenue
Richmond, Virginia 23284
TWX: 710-956-0198
NUC Code: VIRCU
OCLC Code: VRC

Virginia Polytechnic Institute &
State University
Photoduplication Services
Carol M. Newman Library
Blacksburg, Virginia 24060
TWX: 710-875-3690
NUC Code: ViBlbV

Virginia State Library
Richmond, Virginia 23219
TWX: 710-956-004
NUC Code: Vi

Virginia State College
Johnston Memorial Library
Petersburg, Virginia 23803
TWX: 710-957-2334
NUC Code: VIPETS

Virginia Union University
William J. Clark Library
1500 N. Lombardy Street
Richmond, Virginia 23220

WASHINGTON

Seattle Public Library
Interlibrary Loans
1000 Fourth Avenue
Seattle, Washington 98104
NUC Code: WaS

Washington State Library
Interlibrary Loans
Olympia, Washington 98104
NUC Code: Wa

Washington State Historical Society
315 No. Stadium Way
Tacoma, Washington 98403

Washington State University
Libraries
Interlibrary Loans
Pullman, Washington 99164
TWX: 510-774-1091
NUC Code: WaPS

University of Washington
Central Microfilm Unit
Library, FM-25
Seattle, Washington 98195

University of Washington
Law Library
Condon Hall JB-20
1100 NE Campus Parkway
Seattle, Washington 98105
NUC Code: WaU-L

WEST VIRGINIA

Bethany College
T. W. Phillips Library
Bethany, West Virginia 26032
NUC Code: WVBEC

West Virginia Library Commission
Reference Library
Science & Cultural Center
Charleston, West Virginia 25305
TWX: 1-710-930-8767
NUC Code: Wv

W. Va. Department of Archives &
History
Science and Cultural Center
Capitol Complex
Charleston, West Virginia 25305

West Virginia Institute of
Technology
Vining Library
Montgomery, West Virginia 25136
TWX: 710-938-1623

West Virginia University Library
Interlibrary Loan Department
Main Campus
Morgantown, West Virginia 26506
NUC Code: WvU

W. Va. Wesleyan College
A. M. Pfeiffer Library
Buckhannon, West Virginia 26201

WISCONSIN

Marquette University
Interlibrary Loan Service
Memorial Library
1415 W. Wisconsin Avenue
Milwaukee, Wisconsin 53233
TWX: 910-262-3323
NUC Code: WMM

Milwaukee Public Library
814 West Wisconsin Avenue
Milwaukee, Wisconsin 53233

University of Wisconsin—Green Bay
Library
Interlibrary Loan Department
Green Bay, Wisconsin 54302
TWX: 910-263-1280

University of Wisconsin Library
Photoduplication Service
Interlibrary Loan Department
728 State Street
Madison, Wisconsin 53706
NUC Code: WU

University of Wisconsin—Madison
Kurt F. Wendt Library
215 N. Randall Avenue
Madison, Wisconsin 53706
TWX: 910-286-2749

University of Wisconsin—Milwaukee
Interlibrary Loan Office
Library
Milwaukee, Wisconsin 53201
TWX: 910-262-3165
NUC Code: WMUW

University of Wisconsin—Oshkosh
Libraries/Learning Resources
Oshkosh, Wisconsin 54901
TWX: 414-424-1021
NUC Code: WOSHU

University of Wisconsin-Parkside
Library/Learning Center
Interlibrary Loan
Wood Road
Kenosha, Wisconsin 53140
TWX: 910-274-2364
NUC Code: W
OCLC Code: GZP

University of Wisconsin—Stout
Interlibrary Loan
MRS - Pierce Library
Menomonie, Wisconsin 54751
TWX: 910-285-1671
NUC Code: WMenU

Wisconsin   Department   of   Public
Instruction
Division for Library Services
Bureau   for   Reference   and   Loan
Services
3030 Darbo Drive
Madison, Wisconsin 53714
TWX: 910-286-2768
NUC Code: WMaPI-RL

WYOMING

University of Wyoming Libraries
Interlibrary Loan
Laramie, Wyoming 82071
TWX: 910-949-4946
NUC Code: WyU

Wyoming State Library
Interlibrary Loan
Supreme Court Building
Cheyenne, Wyoming 82001
TWX: 910-949-4787
NUC Code: Wy

U.S. TERRITORIES
AND DEPENDENCIES

GUAM

University of Guam
R.F.K. Memorial Library
Circulation Department
Interlibrary Loans
P.O. Box EK
Agana, Guam 96910

PUERTO RICO

University of Puerto Rico
Mayaguez Campus Library
Mayaguez, Puerto Rico 00708

VIRGIN ISLANDS

College of the Virgin Islands
Library
St. Thomas, Virgin Islands 00801

ARGENTINA

Biblioteca Publica de la Universidad
Nacional de la Plata. Centro de
Documentacion, Plaza Rocha No. 137
Argentina Telex: 1351

AUSTRALIA

National Library of Australia
Loans and Locations Service
Canberra A.C.T., Australia 2600

State Library of South Australia
Box 419, G.P.O.
Adelaide, S.A. 5001
Australia
Telex: 82074

AUSTRIA

Osterreichische Nationalbibliothek
Josefsplatz 1
A - 1014 Wien
Austria
Telex: 12624 ONBib.

Universitatsbibliothek Wien
A - 1010 Wien
Dr. Karl Lueger-Ring 1
Austria
Telex: 75619

BULGARIA

Cyril and Methodius National
Library
International Lending Service
Blvd Tolbuhin 11
1504 Sofia
Bulgaria
Telex: 22432 Natlib

CANADA*

Alberta Research Council Library
11315 87 Avenue
Edmonton, Alberta T8N2L2

Legislature Library
Legislative Assembly of Alberta
216 Legislature Building
Edmonton, Alberta
T5K 2B6
NUC Code: CaAEP

University of Alberta
Interlibrary Loans
Library
Edmonton, Alberta T6G 2E1
Telex: 037-2723
NUC Code: CAEU

University of British Columbia Library
Interlibrary Loan
2075 Wesbrook Place
Vancouver, British Columbia
Canada V6T 1W5
Telex: 0453296
Woodward Biomedical Library:
04:508690
NUC Code: CaBVaU

*Entries are arranged alphabetically by provinces and territories, subarranged by names of institutions.

The University of Manitoba
Elizabeth Dafoe Library
Interlibrary Loans
Winnipeg, Manitoba, Canada R3T
2N2
Telex: 07-587721
NUC Code: CaMWU

University of Manitoba,
Dental Library
780 Bannatyne Avenue
Winnipeg, Manitoba, Canada, R3E
OW3

University of New Brunswick
Interlibrary Loans
Harriet Irving Library
P.O. Box 7500
Fredericton, New Brunswick, Canada
E3B 5H5
Telex: 014-46186
NUC Code: Ca NBFU

Memorial University of Newfoundland
Library, Interlibrary Loans
St. John's, Newfoundland, Canada
AIC 5S7
Telex: 016-4677
NUC Code: NfSM

Dalhousie University
Killam Memorial Library
Halifax, Nova Scotia, Canada B3H 4H

Nova Scotia Technical College
Library
P.O. Box 1000
Halifax, Nova Scotia, Canada
B3J 2X4
NUC Code: CaNSHT

Saint Mary's University
Patrick Power Library
Halifax, Nova Scotia
B3H 3C3
NUC Code: CaNSHS

Atomic Energy of Canada Limited
Technical Information Branch
Chalk River Nuclear Laboratories
Chalk River, Ontario, Canada
KOJ 1JO
Telex: 053-34555
NUC Code: CaOcKa

Canada Institute for Scientific &
Technical Information
National Research Council of
Canada
Ottawa, Canada K1A OS2
Telex: 053-3115
NUC Code: CaOON

Carleton University
Interlibrary Loans
The Library
Colonel By Drive
Ottawa, Ontario Canada
K1S 5B6
Telex: 053-4232
NUC Code: CaOOCC

McMaster University
Mills Memorial Library
Hamilton, Ontario, Canada L8S 4L6
Telex: 061-8640
NUC Code: CaOHM

Metropolitan Toronto Central Library
789 Yonge Street
Toronto, Ontario
Canada M4W 2G8
Telex: 06-22232
NUC Code: CaOTMCL
(For older works: CaOTP)

National Library of Canada
Interlibrary Loans
395 Wellington Street
Ottawa, Ontario, Canada
K1A ON4
Telex: 053-4311, 053-4312
NUC Code: CaOONL

Queen's University at Kingston
Douglas Library
Kingston, Ontario
Canada K7L 5CA
Telex: 066-3244
NUC Code: CaOKQ

University of Guelph Library
Guelph, Ontario
Canada N1G 2W1
Telex: 069-56540
NUC Code: CAOGU

University of Western Ontario
Circulation Services
The D. B. Weldon Library
London Ontario
Canada N6A 3K7
Telex: 064-7134
NUC Code: CaOLU

York University
Interlibrary Loans
203C Scott Library
4700 Keele Street, Downsview
Ontario, Canada M3J 2R2
Telex: 06-965502
NUC Code: CaOTY

McGill University
Interlibrary Loans
Reference Department
McLennan Library
3459 McTavish Street
Montreal, P.Q., Canada
H3A 1Y1
Telex: 05-268510

Universite de Montreal
Pret Entre Bibliotheques
C.P. 6128
Succ. A, Montreal
Canada
Telex: 05-267389
TWX: 610-421-3102
NUC Code: CaQMU

DENMARK

Det Kongelige Bibliotek
Christians Brygge 8
Dk-1219, Copenhagen K Denmark

Statsbiblioteket, State & University
Library
Universitetsparken
DK-8000 Arhus C
Denmark
Telex: 64515

EGYPT

American University in Cairo
Library
113, SH. Kasr El Aini
Cairo, Egypt A.R.E.

FINLAND

Helsinki University Library
P.O. Box 312
00171 Helsinki 17
Street addr. Unionink. 36
Finland
Telex: 121538
NUC Code: 6333T

Helsinki University of Technology
Library
Otaniementie 9
SF 02150 ESPOO 15
Finland
Telex: 12-1591

FRANCE

Bibliotheque de la Faculte de
Medecine
12 Rue de l'Ecole de Medecine
75270 Paris Cedex 06
France

Bibliotheque Nationale
Departement de la Phonotheque et
de l'Audiovisuel
Service Micrographie
58 rue de Richelieu
75084 Paris Cedex 02
France

Bibliotheque Nationale
Service Photographique
58 rue Richelieu
75084 Cedex 02 France

Bibliotheque Nationale et
Universitaire de Strasbourg
6, Place de la Republique
B.P. 1029/F
67070 Strasbourg Cedex
France

Universites de Paris
Bibliotheque de l'Institut National
des Langues et Civilisations Orientales
2 rue de Lille, Paris, 75007 France

GERMANY (EAST)

Deutsche Staatsbibliothek
Reprographische Abteilung
DDR 1086 Berlin Unter den Linden
8
Telex: 011 27 57

GERMANY (WEST)

Stadt- und Universitatsbibliothek
Bockenheimer Landstr. 134-138
D 6000 Frankfurt a.M.
Germany
Telex: 414 024

Universitatsbibliothek
Erlangen-Nurnberg
Universitatsstrabe 4
8520 Erlangen
Germany

Universitat Heidelberg
Universitatsbibliothek
Postfach 105749
D 6900 Heidelberg 1
Germany

GHANA

University of Ghana
Balme Library
P.O. Box 24
Legon, Ghana

GREAT BRITAIN

British Library Lending Division
Boston SPA
Wetherby
West Yorkshire
LS 23 7BQ England

The British Library
Reference Division
Photographic Services
Great Russell Street
London WC1B 3DG, England

British Library of Political &
Economic Sciences
London School of Economics and
Political Science
10 Portugal Street
London WC2A 2HD, England

Cambridge University Library
West Road
Cambridge CB3 9DR, England

Durham University Library
Reference Librarian
Palace Green
Durham, DH1 3RN, U.K.

Edinburgh University
Library
George Square
Edinburgh EH8 9LJ
Scotland

India Office Library and Records
197 Blackfriars Road
London SE1 8NG, Great Britain

Manchester Central Library
St. Peters SQ M2 5PD
Manchester, England

National Library of Scotland
George IV Bridge
Edinburgh EH1 1EW, Scotland
Telex: 72638

The National Library of Wales
Llyfrgell Genedlaethol Cymru
Aberystwyth, Dyfed, Wales,
SY23, 3BU

School of Oriental and African
Studies
The Library
Malet Street
London SE 13 7NP U.K.

Science Museum Library
London SW7 5NH
England
Telex: 21200

Sciences Reference Library
25 Southampton Buildings
Chancery Lane
London WC2A IAW
England

Wellcome Institute for the
History of Medicine
183 Euston Road
London NW1 2 BP, England
Telex: 22280

University of London Library
Senate House, Malet Street
London, WC1E 7HU, England

HUNGARY

Magyar Tudomanyos Akademia
Konyvtara
/Library of Hungarian Academy of
Sciences/
H-1361 Budapest V.
Akademia utca 2.
Postafiok 7
Hungary

National Szechenyi Library
H-1827 Budapest
Department of Printed Books and
Periodicals Reference Service
Hungary
Telex: H-224226

ICELAND

Haskolabokasafn-University Library
Reykjavik
Iceland

INDIA

Government of India
National Library
Belvedere, Calcutta 700027
India

IRELAND

National Library of Ireland
Kildare Street
Dublin, Ireland

Trinity College
The Library
College Street
Dublin 2, Ireland

ISRAEL

Central Zionist Archives
P.O. Box 92
Jerusalem 91000, Israel

The Jewish National and University
Library
Reprographic Service
P.O.B. 503
Jerusalem, Israel
Telex: 25367
NUC Code: INUL IL

ITALY

Biblioteca Nazionale Centrale
Vittorio Emanuele II
Rome 00185 Italy

Biblioteca Nazionale Marciana
S. Marco 7
30124 Venezia, Italy

Biblioteca Nazionale
Vittorio Emanuele III
Napoli, Italy

JAMAICA

University of the West Indies
Library
Mona, Kingston 7, Jamaica, West
Indies

JAPAN

Kyoto University Library
Yoshida-Honmachi, Sakyo-ku,
606 Kyoto, Japan

National Diet Library
10-1, Nagata-cho 1-chome,
Chiyoda-ku
Tokyo 100 Japan

MALAYSIA

Perpustakaan Negara Malaysia
(National Library of Malaysia)
1st Floor,
Wisma Thakurdas/Wisma Sachdev,
.Jalan Raja Laut,
Kuala Lumpur 02-07
Malaysia

NETHERLANDS

Koninklijke Bibliotheek
Lange Voorhout 34
's-Gravenhage
Netherlands

NEW ZEALAND

The Alexander Turnbull Library
P.O. Box 12349
Wellington, New Zealand
Telex: 3076

University of Auckland
The Reference Librarian
Private Bag,
Auckland, New Zealand
Telex: NZ 21480

NIGERIA

University of Ibadan
Ibadan University Library
Ibadan, Nigeria
Telex: 31233

PANAMA

Universidad de Panama
Direccion de Bibliotecas
Estafeta Universitaria
Panama, R de P.

PERU

Instituto Nacional de Cultura
Biblioteca Nacional
Oficina   de   Investigaciones
Bibliograficas
Laboratorio de Reprografia
Lima, Peru

PHILIPPINES

Ateneo de Manila Libraries
Photoduplication Service
Loyola Heights, Quezon City 3005
Philippines

National Library of the Philippines
T. M. Kalaw Street
Ermita, Manila 2801
Philippines

University of the Philippines Library
Reprographic Services
Gonzalez Hall, Diliman, Quezon
City 3004
Philippines

POLAND

Biblioteka Jagiellonska
AL. Mickiewieza 22
30-059 Krakow, Poland

Biblioteka Narodowa
UL. Hankiewicza 1,
00 973 Warszawa, Poland
Telex: 813702BN PL

PORTUGAL

Biblioteca Geral DA Universidade
Coimbra, Portugal

Biblioteca Nacional de Lisboa
R. Ocidental ao Campo Grande no.
83, Lisboa, Portugal

RHODESIA

National Archives of Rhodesia
Private Bag 7729
Causeway, Rhodesia

RUMANIA

Biblioteca Centrala universitara,
Bucuresti,
Str. Onesti nr. 1,
Sectorul 1, Romania

SINGAPORE

National Library
Reference Services Division
Stamford Road
Singapore 6 REP. Singapore
Telegraphic   add: NATLIB
SINGAPORE

SOUTH AFRICA

University of Singapore Library
Microfilm Services Department
Bukit Timah Rd. Singapore 10

CSIR Library, CSTI
P.O. Box 395
Pretoria, Republic of South Africa
0001
Telex: 3-630

The South African Library
Queen Victoria Street
Cape Town
8001 South Africa

University of the Witwatersrand
Library
P.O. Box 31550
Braamfontein, South Africa 2017
Telex: S.A. 87330

SPAIN

Biblioteca Nacional
Avenida de Calvo Sotelo, 20
Madrid-1 (Espana)

Centro Nacional de Microfilm
c/Serrano, no 115 - Madrid-6
(Espana)

Enrique   Esteve   Garcia—Textile
Library
Ave. Jose Antonio, 12
ALCOY. Alicante. Spain

SRI LANKA

National Museum Library
Department of National Museums
P.O. Box 854
Colombo-7, Sri Lanka

SWEDEN

Goteborgs Universitetsbibliotek,
Centralbiblioteket
Box 5096
S-402 22 Goteborg, Sweden
Telex: 20896 UBGBG S

Goteborgs Universitetsbibliotek
(Biomedical Library)
Fack, 400 33 Goteborg 33
Sweden

Kungl. biblioteket/
The Royal Library
Reprogr. sect.
Box 5039
S-102 41 Stockholm 5
Sweden
Telex: 1640 KBS S

Kungl. Tekniska
Hogskolans Bibliotek
Royal Institute of Technology
S-100 44 Stockholm, Sweden
Telex: 10389 KTHB S

University Library
Interlibrary Loan Service
Box 1010
221 03 Lund 1
Sweden

Uppsala universitetsbibliotek
Reprosektionen
Box 510
S-751 20 UPPSALA, Sweden
Address for loan requests:
Uppsala universitetsbibliotek
Laneexpeditionen
Box 510
S-751 20 UPPSALA, Sweden
Telex: 76076 UB UPPS S

SWITZERLAND

Swiss National Library
Hallwylstrasse 15
3003 Bern, Switzerland

TAIWAN

National Central Library
43 Nan Hai Road
Taipei, Taiwan
Republic of China

TURKEY

Istanbul Universitesi:
Kutuphanesi
Istanbul, Beyazit
Takvimhane Cad. No. 15
Turkey

UNITED NATIONS

United Nations Dag Hammarskjold
Library
UN Plaza
New York, New York 10017

VATICAN

La Biblioteca Apostolica Vaticana
Laboratorio Fotografico
Vatican City State

VENEZUELA

Bibliotheca Nacional de Venezuela
Bolsa a San Francisco
Caracas 101
Venezuela
NUC Code: APENTADO 6525

International Labour Documentation: Cumulative Catalogue of the ILO Library, 1965-1977

The collection covers 136 COM microfiches (A6 format: 105 mm x 148 mm; 4" x 6"; each 400 frames, 48x reduction) computer-produced cumulation with approximately 72,000 abstracts at the price of 550 Sw.frs.

The International Labour Documentation is a bibliographical record based on current acquisitions in the ILO Central Library, covering the fields of industrial relations, management, manpower planning, vocational training and other problems of economic and social development. The Cumulative Catalogue 1965-77 contains 54,000 pages with 72,000 abstracts and indexes and comprises a master file of abstracts, a subject index, a personal author index, a corporate author index and a title index.

Title List of ILO Publications and Documents, 1970-1977

4 COM microfiches (A6 format: 105 mm x 148 mm; 4" x 6"; each 400 frames; 48x reduction) at the price of 25 Sw.frs.

An indispensable reference tool for all librarians and researchers interested in the field of industrial relations, management, manpower planning, vocational training and other problems of economics and social development. It includes sales publications, mimeographed documents and journal articles. Gives bibliographical information only.

Register of Periodicals in the ILO Library

The volume covers 4 COM microfiches (A6 format: 105 mm x 148 mm; 4" x 6"; each 400 frames; 48x reduction) at the price of 25 Sw.frs.

The register contains a listing by title and by country of some 8,000 periodicals and annual publications currently received by the library of the International Labour Office. In addition, a further 3,000 titles of items no longer received or published are included.

Year Book of Labour Statistics 1935-36 to 1977

The collection of 37 volumes in microfiche form A6 (105 mm x 148 mm; 4" x 6") at the price of 1,070 Sw.frs. *Further volumes in preparation.*

The ILO *Year Book of Labour Statistics* is a unique reference work which brings together in statistical form world-wide data on labour and conditions of work. It provides the background information essential to a proper understanding of trends and developments in labour and related matters influencing all aspects of modern society.

The information given in successive editions from the first issue (1935-36) constitutes an historical review of the changes and trends in the labor situation through the many crises which have shaken the world since the First World War. The main topics covered are: total and economically active population; employment; unemployment; hours of work; household budgets; wages; labour productivity; consumer prices; industrial accidents; industrial disputes.

Minutes of the Governing Body
1919 to 1973 (1st to 190th Sessions)
About 37,500 pages
The collection in microfiche form A6 (105 mm x 148 mm; 4" x 6") at the price of 1,625 Sw.frs. *Further sessions in preparation.*

The Governing Body of the International Labour Office, which is composed of representatives of governments, employers and workers, generally meets every three months. The minutes contain a full account of the discussions of the Governing Body of the ILO, as well as the decisions taken. They thus show not merely what the policy of the Governing Body was at any given time on the most important labour and social questions of the day, but also how that policy was worked out by discussion among the three groups—governments, employers and workers.

Official Bulletin
1920 to 1976 (Vols. I to LIX)
About 30,000 pages
The collection in microfiche form A6 (105 mm x 148 mm; 4" x 6") at the price of 1,340 Sw.frs. *Further volumes in preparation.*

The *Official Bulletin* is the channel through which the International Labour Office supplies official information on matters connected with the life and work of the International Labour Organisation. The material published in the *Official Bulletin* is restricted to such documents and information as are essential to a complete and permanent official record of the history of the Organisation and its work since 1920.

IN PREPARATION ON MICROFICHE

WEP Research Working Papers

WEP Research Working Papers are preliminary research studies circulated to stimulate discussion and critical comment. As such, they are reproduced in limited numbers and given restricted distribution to specialists in the various subject matters covered under the World Employment Programme (income distribution, technology, migration, population, etc.).

This unique collection of some 120 volumes will shortly be available for the first time in microfiche form A6 (105 mm x 148 mm; 4" x 6").

Standing orders for forthcoming volumes are accepted.

For further details please apply directly to:
INTERNATIONAL LABOUR OFFICE
ILO Publications
CH-1211 GENEVA 22
Switzerland.
Telex 22.271

PUBLISHERS MAKE MORE CENTS ON FILM

High costs of material, production, and service are driving most publishers up walls if not out of the business. Others have discovered that Princeton Datafilm is cutting those costs on the order of 80%. Those smart ones are thriving.

Microfilming hundreds of thousands of pages a month for publishers in any and all fields is how we do it.

Microforms are more easily and less expensively duplicated and distributed. Hundreds of copies are available on a few days notice and at a fraction of the cost of paper and postage.

Microforms afford libraries, subscribers, and collectors an opportunity to acquire and store countless more volumes and titles in limited available space. Businesses are finding that they can now establish small outpost branches, each with a full compliment of data resources.

PDF is helping more and more exciting new publishing ventures get off the ground. Ask Law Reprints, Information Resources Press, Congressional Information Service, Clearwater Publishing, or any other micropublishers. Find out more about it. Call or write.

 PRINCETON DATAFILM INCORPORATED
14 Farber Road, Princeton Commerce Center
Box 231, Princeton Junction, NJ 08540
Phone: 609-799-1630

Section III

SUBJECT INDEX

The following index is not a comprehensive subject index, but rather a general guide to broadly selected subjects.

ASIAN STUDIES
  Asia Library Services
  Center for Chinese Research
    Materials Association of Research
    Libraries
  Center for Research Libraries
  Central Asian Research Centre
  The Centre for East Asian Cultural
    Studies
  Fondation Nationale des Sciences
    Politiques
  The Institute for Advanced Studies
    of World Religions
  Publications Orientalistes de France
  Yushodo Film Publications Ltd.

BIBLIOGRAPHY
  Blackwell Bibliographical Services
    Limited
  British Library. Bibliographic
    Services Division
  The Carrollton Press
  Human Relations Area File
  National Library of Australia
  Paris Publications Inc.
  University of London, Institute of
    United States Studies
  J. Whitaker & Sons, Ltd.

BIOLOGY
  Biosciences Information Service
  The Rockefeller University Press

BOTANY
  Inter Documentation Company
  Schierenberg, Dieter B.V.

BLACK STUDIES
  KTO Microform Division
  Tuskegee Institute, Division of
    Behavioral Science Research

BRITISH CULTURE AND HISTORY
  Andronicus Publishing Company
  Chadwyck-Healey Ltd.
  Embryo Publishers
  EP Microform Limited
  Harvester Press Ltd.
  Her Majesty's Stationery Office
  Irish Microforms Ltd.
  Mansell Information/Publishing Ltd.
  Mindata Ltd.
  National Library of Scotland
  Oxford Microform Publications Ltd.
  Public Record Office
  World Microfilms Publications Ltd.
  Scolar Press Ltd.

BUSINESS AND FINANCE
  Disclosure Incorporated
  The Financial Times
  The Foundation Center
  Microforms International Marketing
    Corporation
  National Design Center
  Pick Publishing Corporation
  Predicasts, Inc.

CANADIANA
  Archives Canada Microfiches
  Bibliothèque Nationale du Québec
  Canadian Library Association
  Commonwealth Microfilm Library
  McLaren Micropublishing
  MacLean-Hunter Limited Microfilm
    Services
  Micromedia Limited
  Simon Fraser University

CATALOGS
  Gaylord Bros. Inc.
  Information Design Inc.
  MARC Applied Research Company
  Micrologue, Inc.
  National Microfilm Library
  3M Company
  Time Share Corporation

JOURNALS
American Jewish Periodical Center
AMS Press, Inc.
Bell & Howell Micro Photo Division
Brookhaven Press
J. S. Canner & Company
Consumers' Association
Wm. Dawson & Sons Ltd.
Elsevier Sequoia S.A.
France-Expansion
Gordon and Breach Science
Publishers Ltd.
Greenwood Press, Inc.
Heyden & Son Limited
Immigration History Research
Center
Information Handling Services
Inter Documentation Company
Johnson Associates Inc.
KTO Microform Division
McLaren Micropublishing
Mansell Information/Publishing Ltd.
Microfilm Center, Inc.
Microfilming Corporation of America
Micromedia Limited
Micropublishing International Ltd.
Oxford Microform Publications Ltd.
Pascoe (W & F) Pty. Limited
Plenum Publishing Corporation
Princeton Microfilm Corporation
Springer-Verlag New York Inc.
Swets & Zeitlinger B.V.
Taylor and Francis Ltd.
TV Guide
University Microfilms International
University of Oregon
Wiley-Interscience Journals
The Williams & Wilkins Co.

JUDAICA
American Jewish Periodical Center
Inter Documentation Company

LABOR AND MANAGEMENT
International Labour Office,
Publications
Lomond Publications
Microfilming Corporation of America
State Historical Society of Wisconsin

LATIN AMERICAN STUDIES
Center for Research Libraries
IDAL, Información Documental de
América Latina
Informações, Microformas e
Sistemas

LAW
Butterworths Pty. Ltd.
Commerce Clearing House, Inc.
Congressional Information Service,
Inc.
Environment Information Center
Godfrey Memorial Library
William S. Hein & Co., Inc. Micro-
Film Division
Juta & Company Limited
Law Reprints, Inc.
Meiklejohn Civil Liberties Institute
The Mitchie Company
New York Law Journal
Fred B. Rothman & Co.
Temple University School of Law
Trans-Media
West Publishing Company

LIBRARIES AND LIBRARY SCIENCE
Academic Press, Inc.
American Library Association
British Library. Bibliographic
Services Division
Georgia Institute of Technology
Ingram Book Company

Leeds Polytechnic School of
   Librarianship
The Library of Congress,
   Photoduplication Service
Mansell Information/Publishing Ltd.
MARC Applied Research Company
National Library of Australia
National Microfilm Library
Oxford Microform Publications Ltd.
3M Company

LITERATURE
   General Microfilm Company
   Hill Monastic Manuscript Library
   Information Handling Services
   Library Resources Inc.
   Lost Cause Press
   Micrographics II
   New University Press, Inc.
   Georg Olms Verlag
   Oxford University Press
   Readex Microprint Corp.
   Scholars' Facsimiles & Reprints
   Southern Illinois University Press
   University of Washington Press

LINGUISTICS
   Association for Computational
      Linguistics
   Centre de Préparation
      Documentaire à la Traduction
   France-Expansion
   The Regents Press of Kansas
   Scolar Press Ltd.

MATHEMATICS
   SIAM

MEDICINE
   Aesthetic, Reconstructive, and
      Facial Plastic Surgery
   Chapman & Hall Ltd.
   Excerpta Medica

Gordon and Breach Science
   Publishers Ltd.
Heyden & Son Limited
The New York Microform Journal for
   Medical Archives
Wildlife Disease Association
The Williams & Wilkins Co.

MICROGRAPHICS
   Microfiche Foundation
   Microfilm Association of Great
      Britain
   Microform Review
   Micrographics Australasia
   Microinfo Ltd.
   National Micrographics Association
   The National Reprographic Centre
      for documentation
   Scheffel'sche Verlagsbuchhandlung

MUSIC
   Berandol Music Limited
   Dakota Graphics, Inc.
   Gregg Music Sources
   The Library of Congress,
      Photoduplication Service
   Schnase Microfilm Systems
   Sibley Music Library Microform
      Service
   University Music Editions

NEWSPAPERS
   African Imprint Library Services
   Asia Library Services
   Association Pour la Conservation et
      la Reproduction Photographique
      de la Presse
   Bell & Howell Micro Photo Division
   Bibliothèque Nationale du Québec
   Canadian Library Association
   Caribbean Imprint Library Services
   Center for Chinese Research
      Materials Association of Research
      Libraries

Section IV

GEOGRAPHIC INDEX

Micropublishers are listed alphabetically within states and countries. Reprographic Centers are not included.

UNITED STATES

ALABAMA
Tuskegee Institute, Division of
Behavioral Science Research

ARIZONA
Americana Unlimited

CALIFORNIA
American Astronautical Society
Association for Computational
Linguistics
California State Library
Gregg Music Sources
Hoover Institution Press
Information Design Inc.
Library Microfilms
Meiklejohn Civil Liberties Institute
Micrographic Publication Service
National Microfilm Library
NICEM
The Stanford University Libraries
Univelt Inc.
Updata Publications, Inc.
Women's History Research Center

COLORADO
Dakota-Graphics, Inc.
Information Handling Services
Micrologue, Inc.
State Historical Society of Colorado

CONNECTICUT
Antiquarian and Landmarks Society,
Inc.
Godfrey Memorial Library
Greenwood Press
Human Relations Area File
Johnson Associates Inc.
Microform Review
NewsBank, Inc.
Research Publications, Inc.
Yale University Library

DELAWARE
Scholarly Resources, Inc.

DISTRICT OF COLUMBIA
American Association for the
Advancement of Science
American Chemical Society

Brookhaven Press
The Catholic University of
America Press, Inc.
Center for Chinese Research
Materials
Congressional Digest Corporation
Congressional Information Service,
Inc.
Congressional Quarterly
Educational Information Services,
Inc.
Educational Resources Information
Center
Information Resources Press
The Library of Congress,
Photoduplication Service
MARC Applied Research Company
National Historical Publications
and Records Commission
United States Government Printing
Office
U.S. National Archives and
Records Service
University Publications of America,
Inc.

GEORGIA
Georgia Institute of Technology

ILLINOIS
American Library Association
Center for Research Libraries
Commerce Clearing House, Inc.
Gas Chromatography Service
Illinois State Historical Library
Library Resources Inc.
New University Press, Inc.
Precedent Publishing, Inc.
Southern Illinois University Press
The University of Chicago Press

INDIANA
The Frederic Luther Company

IOWA
University of Iowa
Wildlife Disease Association

KANSAS
The Regents Press of Kansas

KENTUCKY
Data Courier, Inc.
Lost Cause Press

MARYLAND
Computer Science Press, Inc.
Dataflow Systems, Inc.
Disclosure Incorporated
Lomond Publications
Maryland Historical Society
National Micrographics Association
The Williams & Wilkins Co.

MASSACHUSETTS
Aesthetic, Reconstructive, and
Facial Plastic Surgery
J. S. Canner and Company
General Microfilm Company
Graphic Microfilm, Inc.
Harvard University Press
Massachusetts Historical Society

MICHIGAN
American Concrete Institute
University Microfilms International

MINNESOTA
Hill Monastic Manuscript Library
Immigration History Research
Center
Minnesota Historical Society
3M Company
West Publishing Company

MONTANA
Perceptual and Motor Skills/
Psychological Reports

NEW HAMPSHIRE
Dartmouth College Library
New Hampshire Historical Society
Time Share Corporation,
Micropublishing

NEW JERSEY
American Theological Library
Association Board of Microtext
Educational Testing Service
Microfilming Corporation of America
Princeton Datafilm, Inc.
Princeton Microfilm Corporation
Fred B. Rothman & Co.
Somerset House
James T. White and Company

NEW MEXICO
New Mexico State Records Center
and Archives

NEW YORK
Academic Press
African Imprint Library Services
Allerton Press, Inc.
American Institute of Aeronautics
and Astronautics
American Institute of Physics
AMS Press, Inc.
Andronicus Publishing Company,
Inc.
Asia Library Services
Buffalo and Erie County Historical
Society
Alvina Treut Burrows Institute, Inc.
Caribbean Imprint Library Services
Clearwater Publishing Company,
Inc.

Cornell University Department of
Manuscripts and Archives
Creative Microlibraries, Inc.
Datamics
The Dunlap Society
Engineering Index, Inc.
Environment Information Center
Facts on File, Inc.
Fairchild Microfilms
The Foundation Center
Gaylord Bros., Inc.
Walter de Gruyter, Inc.
William S. Hein & Co., Inc.
The Institute for Advanced Studies
of World Religions
Institute of Electrical and Electronics
Engineers
International Microform Distribution
Service
KTO Microform Division
Law Reprints, Inc.
Microfiche Publications
Microforms International Marketing
Corporation
National Design Center
New York Law Journal
The New York Microform Journal for
Medical Archives
New York Public Library
The New York Times Information
Bank
Jeffrey Norton Publishers, Inc.
Olympic Media Information
Oxford University Press
Paris Publications, Inc.
Pick Publishing Corporation
Plenum Publishing Corporation
Readex Microprint Corp.
The Rockefeller University Press
Franklin D. Roosevelt Library
Schnase Microfilm Systems
Scholars' Facsimiles & Reprints
Sibley Music Library Microform
Service
Springer-Verlag New York Inc.
State University of New York Press

Centre de Préparation
  Documentaire à la Traduction
Fondation Nationale des Sciences
  Politiques
France-Expansion
Institut d'Ethnologie. Museum
  National d'Histoire Naturelle
Microéditions Hachette
Micro-Urba
Publications Gerard Monfort
Publications Orientalistes de France
Service International de Microfilms

IRELAND
Irish Microforms Ltd.

JAPAN
The Centre for East Asian Cultural
Studies
Yushodo Film Publications, Ltd.

THE NETHERLANDS
Excerpta Medica
Microfiche Foundation
Schierenberg, Dieter B.V.
Swets & Zeitlinger B.V.

SCOTLAND
Edinburgh University Press
Embryo Publishers
National Library of Scotland

SOUTH AFRICA
Juta & Company, Limited
Microfile Limited
The Pretoria State Library

SWITZERLAND
Elsevier Sequoia S.A.
Inter Documentation Company AG
International Labour Office,
  Publications
International Trade Centre

WEST GERMANY
Mikrofilmarchiv der
  Deutschsprachigen Presse E.V.
Mikropress GmbH
Georg Olms Verlag GmbH
Verlag Dokumentation, Publishers

U.S. Federal, state, municipal & foreign publications

(on microforms)

Congressional Information Service is, today, the preeminent commercial indexer and micropublisher of government documents. Modern finding aids, in printed and computerized form, serve to quickly and conclusively identify specific information. And, to ensure successful completion of the research process, CIS also provides rigorously organized reproductions of source material in microformat. These are compact, easy to use, and of archival quality, enhancing the investment benefits of already valuable resources.

Congressional Information Service, Inc.
7101 Wisconsin Avenue, Suite 900
Washington, D.C. 20014

Section V

MERGERS & ACQUISITIONS

The following organizations that appeared in *Microform Market Place 76/77* have discontinued micropublishing, merged, been acquired or changed names since publication of the previous edition.

DISCONTINUED

American Petroleum Institute
Communications/Media Productions
EDUCOM, Interuniversity Communications Council
Four Continent Book Corporation
Information Dynamics Corporation
National Congressional Analysis Corporation
Redgrave Information Resources Corporation
Unipub, Inc.

ACQUIRED

Greenwood Press, 51 Riverside Ave., Westport, CT 06880 acquired by
 Congressional Information Service, Inc., 7101 Wisconsin Ave.,
 Washington, DC 20014.

CHANGED NAMES

Antiquariaat Junk to Schierenberg, Dieter B.V., Amsteldijk 44 Amsterdam,
 The Netherlands.
Pollution Abstracts/Oceanic Abstracts to Data Courier, Inc., 620 South Fifth
 Street, Louisville, KY 40202.
The University Press of Kansas to The Regents Press of Kansas, 366 Watson
 Library, Lawrence, KS 66045.
Xerox University Microfilms to University Microfilms International, 300 N. Zeeb
 Road, Ann Arbor, MI 48106.

Section VI

ORGANIZATIONS

The following organizations are actively concerned with educational aspects of the use of microforms in the library environment.

AMERICAN LIBRARY ASSOCIATION
50 East Huron St., Chicago, IL 60601

The American Library Association has two annual conventions. Various committees within the ALA are concerned with the use of microforms. The name of each committee is listed.

Micropublishing

Reprinting

Reproduction of Library Materials Sections

Standards

Policy and Research

Standards for Microfilming Library Card Catalogs

AMERICAN NATIONAL STANDARDS INSTITUTE
1430 Broadway, New York, NY 10018

The American National Standards Institute issues USA Standards in a variety of categories including micrographics. A USA Standard is intended as a guide to aid the manufacturer, the consumer, and the general public.

AMERICAN SOCIETY FOR INFORMATION SCIENCE (ASIS)
1140 Connecticut Ave., N.W., Washington, DC 20036

ASIS has a special interest group for Reprographic Technology and has an annual Convention.

COUNCIL ON LIBRARY RESOURCES
One Dupont Circle, Washington, DC 20036

The Council on Library Resources sponsors research projects in a number of library fields, including the use of microforms and micrographics equipment.

MICROFILM ASSOCIATION OF GREAT BRITAIN
1 and 2 Trinity Churchyard, High St. Guildford, Surrey, England.

The Microfilm Association of Great Britain is a trade association. *Microdoc*, the journal of the association contains articles and news items of interest to librarians. MAGB has several publications on subjects affecting users and potential users of micrographic goods and services.

MICROFORM REVIEW
520 Riverside Ave., P.O. Box 405 Saugatuck Station, Westport, CT 06880

An annual Library Microform Conference is co-sponsored each year by Microform Review and the Bookdealer-Library Relations Committee and Micropublishing Projects Committee of the American Library Association.

NATIONAL MICROGRAPHICS ASSOCIATION
8728 Colesville Rd., Silver Spring, MD 20910

The National Micrographics Association is a trade association. The NMA has two annual meetings and publishes a journal—*The Journal of Micrographics.* Various publications are available from the NMA dealing with micrographics equipment and its use. The NMA has several standards committees. The name of each committee is listed.

Microfiche of Documents

Inspection & Quality Control

Operational Practices

Public Records

Equipment

Microfacsimile

Terminology

Information Storage and Retrieval

Newspapers

Reduction Ratios

COM Format and Coding

NATIONAL REPROGRAPHIC CENTRE FOR DOCUMENTATION
  Hatfield Polytechnic, Endymion Rd. Annexe, Hatfield, Herts, AL 10
  8AU, England

The National Reprographic Centre for documentation is a government
sponsored organization devoted to the study of reprographics. NRCd
publishes a journal, Reprographic Quarterly (formerly, NRCd Bulletin),
and offers equipment evaluation reports and an inquiry service.

Section VII

BIBLIOGRAPHY OF PRIMARY SOURCES

This short annotated list is directed toward the microform user faced with the problem of making a decision concerning some aspect of microforms or microform equipment. No claim is made that all primary sources have been listed, but we believe that the publications cited below will answer many of the basic questions asked by librarians concerning microforms, microform sources, and microform equipment.

A. GENERAL

Hawken, William R. *COPYING METHODS MANUAL*. Chicago: Library Technology Program, American Library Association, 1966.

Covers reproduction processes in general and gives considerable space to microforms, describing each format. A comprehensive, well illustrated work, with an annotated bibliography. Out of print.

LaHood, Charles G., Jr. and Robert C. Sullivan. *REPROGRAPHIC SERVICES IN LIBRARIES: ORGANIZATION AND ADMINISTRATION*. Chicago, Library Technology Program, American Library Association, 1975.

This well-balanced guide to the planning, organization and administration of library reprographic services provides "general guidelines and policy considerations rather than detailed operating instructions." In addition to discussing the state of the art, the book reviews both the scope of duplicating services that could be provided by small, medium and large libraries and administrative aspects of reprography. Appendices provide a great deal of useful information including a list of major photographic standards and sample forms. The book also includes a glossary, well-selected bibliography and index. It is available from Order Department, ALA, 50 East Huron St., Chicago, IL 60611 for $4.50.

LIBRARY RESOURCES & TECHNICAL SERVICES. v. 16, no. 2-; Spring 1972-. Fulton, Mo.: American Library Association. Quarterly.

Micrographic events, products and literature of the past year are reviewed and analyzed in the spring or summer issues. To date Francis F. Spreitzer and Paul A. Napier contributed articles entitled "Developments in Copying, Micrographics and Graphic Communications" (1972:135; 1973:147; 1974:155; 1976:236; and 1977:187) and Carl M. Spaulding and Judy H. Fair contributed an article entitled "Micrographics 1974" (1975:206). Extensive references follow each article.

MICROFORMS AND LIBRARY CATALOGS. Albert Diaz, editor. Westport, Conn.: Microform Review, 1978.

Provides basic readings on how microforms are being utilized *vis-a-vis* library catalogs. It includes information on procedures, alternatives, prices, equipment, and user reaction. The emphasis is on what has been done and reported to date, rather than on the theoretical. Available from Microform Review Inc., 520 Riverside Ave., P.O. Box 405 Saugatuck Station, Westport, CT 06880 for $18.95.

MICROFORMS IN LIBRARIES: A READER. Albert Diaz, editor. Weston, Conn: Microform Review, 1975.

A basic reader that contains articles on all aspects of the usage of microforms in libraries. Available from Microform Review Inc., 520 Riverside Ave., P.O. Box 405 Saugatuck Station, Westport, CT 06880 for $17.50.

MICROFORM RESEARCH COLLECTIONS: A GUIDE. Suzanne Dodson, editor. Westport, Conn: Microform Review, 1978.

A detailed guide describing the contents and associated indexes or bibliographies of 200 microform collections from publishers worldwide. There is a subject-catchword index to all materials described. Available from Microform Review Inc., 520 Riverside Ave., P.O. Box 405 Saugatuck Station, Westport, CT 06880 for $35.00.

National Micrographics Association. *INTRODUCTION TO MICROGRAPHICS.* Silver Spring, MD, 1973.

Describes the common formats and equipment used to make and reproduce microforms. Illustrated, glossary. Available from the National Micrographics Association, Suite 1101, 8728 Colesville Road, Silver Spring, MD 20910 for $2.00.

Nitecki, Joseph Z., *DIRECTORY OF LIBRARY REPROGRAPHIC SERVICES/A WORLD GUIDE.* Westport, Conn.: published for the Reproduction of Library Materials Section, RTSD-American Library Association by Microform Review, 1978.

This is the seventh edition of RLMS' *Directory of Institutional Photoduplication Services in the United States,* first published in 1959. Provides information in tabular format about the reprographic services of over 600 different photoduplication departments in the United States and abroad. It also includes a glossary of terms, rules for requesting reprographic services and a sample library photoduplication order form. Available from Microform Review, Inc., 520 Riverside Ave., P.O. Box 405 Saugatuck Station, Westport, CT 06880 for $12.95.

Rice, E. Stevens. *FICHE AND REEL.* Revised. Ann Arbor: Xerox University Microfilms, 1976.

This free booklet is well illustrated and designed to answer the questions on scholarly micropublishing that are frequently asked by librarians, educators, scholars, and others. Available from University Microfilms International, 300 North Zeeb Rd., Ann Arbor, MI 48106.

Spigai, Francis G. *THE INVISIBLE MEDIUM: THE STATE OF THE ART OF MICROFORM AND A GUIDE TO THE LITERATURE.* Washington, D.C., ERIC in cooperation with the ASIS Special Interest Group on Reprographic Technology, 1973.

This Educational Resources Information Center paper covers aspects of micropublication, provides an overview of equipment, and contains a selected guide to the micrographic literature. Available from the American Society for Information Science, Suite 804, 1140 Connecticut Avenue NW, Washington, D.C. 20036 for $3.50.

Spreitzer, Francis F. "Library microform facilities." *Library Technology Reports*, v. 12, no. 4; July 1976.

A discussion of the microform systems of four libraries, from acquisition and cataloging to the layout, equipment, furnishings, and operation of the microform reading room area. Including photographs and floorplans.

STUDIES IN MICROPUBLISHING: A READER. Allen B. Veaner, editor. Westport, Conn.: Microform Review, 1977.

The historical and administrative aspects of library microforms. Provides a selection of non-technical papers covering a period of 125 years. Available from Microform Review Inc., 520 Riverside Ave., P.O. Box 405 Saugatuck Station, Westport, CT 06880 for $22.50.

Veaner, Allen B. *THE EVALUATION OF MICROPUBLICATIONS: A HANDBOOK FOR LIBRARIANS.* Chicago: Library Technology Program, American Library Association, 1971.

Written specifically for librarians responsible for acquiring and/or evaluating micropublications. Treats aspects of microreproduction, micropublishing practices, and methods for evaluating microforms. Available from American Library Association, 50 East Huron Street, Chicago, Illinois 60611 for $3.25.

B. EQUIPMENT

GUIDE TO MICROGRAPHIC EQUIPMENT. Silver Spring, Md.: National
  Microfilm Association, 1975.

This is the sixth edition of the NMA's *Guide to Microreproduction Equipment*,
first published in 1959. Issued in three parts: Production Equipment; COM
Recorders; and User Equipment. An essential reference tool for information
on specifications and capabilities of cameras, readers, reader/printers,
processors, contact printers, enlargers, accessories, computer output
microfilm (COM), and specialized microform retrieval systems. The
information supplied is descriptive rather than evaluative. Available for $22.00
to members and for $32.00 to non-members from National Micrographics
Association, 8728 Colesville Road, Silver Spring, Md. 20910. The 1976
supplement to the *Guide* is available from the same address for $7.50 to
members and $9.50 to non-members.

Hawken, William R. *EVALUATING MICROFICHE READERS: A HANDBOOK
  FOR LIBRARIANS.* Washington DC.: Council on Library Resources, 1975.

Pages of various library materials are reprinted in the book. The same material
is also microreduced at a ratio of 20:1 and 24:1 and furnished on two positive
and two negative microfiche. Anyone, without any technical knowledge of the
field, may insert the fiche in the reader being examined and conduct a legibility
test using the full-sized reprint in the book as a benchmark. An introductory
essay provides guidelines. Distributed to the major research libraries in the
United States. Out of print.

LIBRARY TECHNOLOGY REPORTS. 1965-. Chicago: American Library
  Association. Six times a year.

A full section is dedicated to ongoing objective evaluation of microform readers
and reader/printers. Compilations of retrieval equipment into tabular form are
helpful in making comparisons. Evaluations are extensive and cover areas
such as operator-machine relationships and hazards in addition to those one
would normally expect. Published in a loose-leaf format during 1965-1975.
The annual subscription is $125.00 from American Library Association, 50
East Huron Street, Chicago, Illinois 60611. An edited backfile for the 1965-
1975 period entitled the *Sourcebook of Library Technology,* is available on
microfiche for $50.00 ($25.00 for current LTR subscribers) from the same
address.

MICROGRAPHICS EQUIPMENT REVIEW. 1976-. Westport, Conn.:
  Microform Review. Quarterly.

Concentrates on the subjective evaluation of microform equipment, based
upon the authority, expertise, insight and reputation of its editors, first William
R. Hawken, and now William Saffady. Annual subscription prices vary from
$85.00 to $125.00 depending on the size of the subscribing library's book and
periodical budget. Available from Microform Review Inc., 520 Riverside Ave.,
P.O. Box 405 Saugatuck Station, Westport, CT 06880.

C. BIBLIOGRAPHY

DISSERTATION ABSTRACTS INTERNATIONAL. 1938-. Ann Arbor, Mich.:
   University Microfilms. Monthly.

The most comprehensive listing of United States, and since July 1969 also
foreign, mostly European, doctoral dissertations and selected masters' theses
reduced to microform from over 300 universities. First published as *Microfilm
Abstracts* (1938-1951); then as *Dissertation Abstracts* (1952-June 1969).
Since July 1966 issued in two sections: A; the humanities and social sciences,
and B; the sciences and engineering. Cumulative author, title, and subject
indices of over 500,000 titles complement the abstracts. The subject index
follows the subject heading system of the Library of Congress. Annual
subscription $175.00 (U.S. and Canada) from University Microfilms, P.O. Box
1764, Ann Arbor, Michigan 48106; and $295.00 (international) from University
Microfilms International, 18 Bedford Row, London, United Kingdom WC1R
4EJ.

GUIDE TO MICROFORMS IN PRINT. 1961-. Westport, Conn.: Microform
   Review. Annual.

Provides bibliographic access to microform titles available worldwide. All
entries, domestic and non-U.S., are interfiled to provide a comprehensive
author/title listing. Over 70,000 titles are listed with format and purchase
information. Available from Microform Review Inc., 520 Riverside Ave., P.O.
Box 405 Saugatuck Station, Westport, CT 06880 for $42.50. ($35.00 for
standing order customers.)

MICROFORM REVIEW. 1972-. Westport, Conn.: Microform Review. Six
   times a year.

A library oriented publication, devoted to current news about microforms.
Issues usually include 4-6 articles, comments, reviews of major microfilming
projects, and a cumulative author-title index to microform reviews. Annual
subscription $35.00 from Microform Review, Inc., P.O. Box 405 Saugatuck
Station, Westport, Connecticut 06880, in either inkprint or in microfiche; and
$50.00 for both formats. A cumulative index for the years 1972-1976 is
available for $12.95 from the same address.

NATIONAL REGISTER OF MICROFORM MASTERS. 1965-. Washington
    D.C.: Library of Congress. Annual.

A comprehensive union catalog listing the master microform holdings of some
300 U.S. and foreign libraries and commercial producers of microforms.
Included are foreign and domestic books, pamphlets, serials and foreign
doctoral dissertations. Excluded are technical reports, typescript translations,
foreign or domestic archival manuscript collections, newspapers, U.S.
doctoral dissertations, and masters' theses. A six-volume cumulative edition,
published in 1976, supersedes all previous editions through 1975. Arranged
alphabetically by main entry it lists over 320,000 titles including some 70,000
serials. The annuals, published in the spring of the following year, contain ca.
50,000 new entries each. Available from Cataloging Distribution Service,
Library of Congress, Washington, D.C. 20541, as follows:

1965-1975	$190.00
1976	35.00
1977	In preparation

NATIONAL UNION CATALOG OF MANUSCRIPT COLLECTIONS. 1959/61-.
    Washington D.C.: Library of Congress. Annual.

The most comprehensive cooperative catalog of manuscript collections
reported by some 990 U.S. repositories. Since its inception to date, some
38,000 manuscript collections are listed, including the original and/or the
microform copies. Indices, cumulated at various intervals, provide
supplemental information on nearly 400,000 topical subjects, and personal,
family, corporate and geographical names. Available from Cataloging
Distribution Service, Library of Congress, Washington, D.C. 20541, unless
otherwise noted, as follows:
    1959-1961. Out-of-print. Positive microfilm $10.99; electrostatic photocopy
        (unbound) $58.00 from Photoduplication Service, Library of Congress,
        Washington, D.C. 20540.
    1962 and Index 1959-62 $13.50 from Shoestring Press, Inc., 995 Sherman
        Avenue, Hamden, Connecticut 06541.

1963-64 and Index 1963-64	$10.00
1965 and Index 1963-1965	15.00
1966 and Index 1963-1966	15.00
1967 and Index 1967	15.00
1968 and Index 1967-68	25.00
1969 and Index 1967-69	50.00
1970 and Index 1970	50.00

1971 and Index 1970-71	50.00
1972 and Index 1970-72	50.00
1973-74 and Index 1970-74	50.00
1975 and Index 1975	50.00
1976 and Index 1975-76	60.00
1977 and Index 1975-77	In preparation

NEWSPAPER AND GAZETTE REPORT. 1973-. Washington D.C.: Library of
Congress. Three Times a year.

A singular source devoted to two special catagories of serials. Edited by Imre
T. Jármy, Newspaper Microfilming Coordinator, and published by the Library
of Congress, it reports on current developments in the location, microfilming,
preservation, and bibliographic control of newspapers and foreign official
gazettes. Began publication as *Foreign Newspaper Report* (1973); changed
title to *Foreign Newspaper and Gazette Report* (1974-1975). Articles
published describe the preservation and other activities of the Library of
Congress as well as several domestic and foreign institutions. Supplements
the *National Register of Microform Masters* (for gazettes) and *Newspapers in
Microform* by publishing "intent to microfilm" statements submitted by various
domestic and foreign institutions and by reporting on title changes, mergers,
absorptions, and other pertinent information within its scope. Beginning in
1977, the December issue includes an annual index. Available on a need-to-
know basis to members and committees of Congress, libraries and other
organizational units of institutions of higher learning, firms, societies,
foundations, and publishers, as well as religious, labor, and other special and
public libraries from Central Services Division, Library of Congress,
Washington, D.C. 20540. A cumulative index for the years 1973-1976 is also
available from the same address.

NEWSPAPERS IN MICROFORM. 1973-. Washington D.C.: Library of
  Congress. Annual.

The best single source of information on newspapers which are reduced to
microform. A cumulative edition published in 1973 and in two volumes entitled:
Newspapers in Microform: United States, 1948-1972, and *Newspapers in
Microform: Foreign Countries, 1948-1972,* is the seventh edition of
Newspapers on Microfilm, first published in 1948. Arranged alphabetically by
state or country, city, and title, it lists the master as well as the service
microforms of 34,289 U.S. and 8,620 foreign titles held by some 1,200
domestic and foreign libraries and commercial producers of microforms.
Annual supplements, published in one volume and in the spring of the
following year, contain ca. 2,500 titles each and complement the 1948-1972
edition. A 1973-1977 quinquennial edition in two volumes is under preparation
in lieu of the 1977 annual supplement. Available from Cataloging Distribution
Service, Library of Congress, Washington, D.C. 20541, as follows:

Foreign Countries, 1948-1972	$10.00
1973-1977	In preparation
United States, 1948-72	30.00
1973-77	In preparation
1973	11.25
1974	13.25
1975	15.75
1976	16.00

SUBJECT GUIDE TO MICROFORMS IN PRINT. 1961-. Westport, Conn:
  Microform Review. Annual.

Microform editions of books, journals, newspapers, bulletins, reports,
collections, art facsimiles, illustrations, catalogs, and bibliographies are listed
under 135 subject classifications derived from the Library of Congress,
Subject Classification Division, *Outline of the Library of Congress
Classification,* 3rd ed. (Washington, 1975). This subject listing is generated
from the entries in *Guide to Microforms in Print.*
   *Available from Microform Review Inc., 520 Riverside Ave., Saugatuck
Station, Westport, CT 06880 for $42.50. ($35.00 for standing order
customers.)*

There are times when the CFR makes you wish you never heard of government documents.

We're aware of your problems. We understand how frustrating government documents can be, and how a search can quickly use up your time when you have other things to do.

We can help you! We've taken the drudgery and uncertainty out of working with government documents and legal publications. Our business is information management and distribution. We organize and index information so that you can quickly and easily locate and retrieve a single, needed document from among thousands or even millions of pages on file. Our latest project, for example, is indexing the *Code of Federal Regulations.*

Our extensive data base of government and legal information includes such collections as the *Federal Register, U.S. Statutes at Large,* the *Congressional Record, State Session Laws* and many others. Because they're segmented, you can order them according to your specialized needs.

To learn more about how we can help you, call our toll-free number today, or better yet, use the coupon to receive your copy of a colorful wall chart that visually traces the history of each *CFR* title through name changes and reserved status. We hope the chart will be the first of many ways we'll be able to make you feel good about government documents.

For information, call toll-free: 1-800-821-3424, Ext. 279
In Missouri: 1-800-892-7655, Ext. 279

Information Handling Services
An Indian Head Company

Section VIII

CALENDAR 1978-1979

The conferences, meetings, and seminars listed in this section are most likely to be of interest to the purchaser of micropublications.

1978

MAY   9-12   27th Annual Conference and Exposition of the National Micrographics Association, Boston, MA

             21-24 American Society for Information Science 7th Mid-Year Meeting, Houston, TX

JUNE   24-30 American Library Association Annual Conference, Chicago, Il

SEPT.   17-22 10th International Micrographic Congress and Exhibition, Johannesburg, South Africa

OCTOBER   11-13 Fourth Annual Library Microform Conference, Sponsored by the Micropublishing Projects Committee, RTSD-American Library Association, Bookdealer-Library Relations Committee, RTSD-American Library Association, and Microform Review Inc., Washington, DC

             31-Nov. 2 National Micrographics Association Midyear Meeting, Seattle, WA

NOVEMBER   13-17   American Society for Information Science 41st
Annual Conference, New York, NY

1979

JANUARY   21-27   American Library Association Midwinter Meeting,
Chicago, IL

MAY   8-11   28th Annual Conference and Exposition of the
National Micrographics Association, Atlanta, GA

JUNE   24-30 American Library Association Annual Conference,
Dallas, TX

OCTOBER   14-18 American Society for Information Science 42nd
Annual Conference, Minneapolis, MN

NOVEMBER   1-2   Fifth Annual Library Microform Conference,
Sponsored by the Micropublishing Projects
Committee, RTSD-American Library Association,
Bookdealer-Library Relations Committee, RTSD-
American Library Association and Microform
Review Inc., Boston, MA

            7-9   National Micrographics Association Midyear
Meeting, San Antonio, TX

Section IX

NAMES & NUMBERS

A

Academic Microforms Inc., 1317 Filbert St., Philadelphia, PA 19107. 215/563-4040.

Academic Press, Inc., 111 Fifth Ave., New York, NY 10003. 212/741-6800.

Adam, Ena, Gordon and Breach Science Publishers Ltd., 41/42 William IV Street, London WC2 England. (01) 836-5125.

Adler, James B., Congressional Information Service, Inc., 7101 Wisconsin Ave., Washington, DC 20014. 301/654-1550.

Aesthetic, Reconstructive, and Facial Plastic Surgery, 16 Prescott St., Brookline, MA 02146. 617/566-2050.

African Imprint Library Services, Guard Hill Rd., Bedford, NY 10506. 914/234-3752.

Agoston, Istvan, International Trade Centre, Palais des Nations, CH-1211, Genève 10, Switzerland. 31-12-55.

Aitchison, T. M., INSPEC, Savoy Place, London WC2R OBL England. (01) 240-1871.

Albert, S. C., World Microfilms Publications Ltd., 62 Queen's Grove, London NW8 6ER, England. (01) 586-3092.

Alderfer, William K., Illinois State Historical Library, Old State Capitol, Springfield, IL 62706. 217/782-4836.

Alexander, A. W., National Technical Information Service, 5285 Port Royal Road, Springfield, VA 22161. 703/557-4734.

Allerton Press, Inc., 150 Fifth Ave. New York, NY 10011. 212/924-3950.

Alrich S. G., The Michie Company, P.O. Box 57, Charlottesville, VA 22902. 804/295-6171.

American Association for the Advancement of Science, 1515 Massachusetts Ave., N.W., Washington, DC 20005. 202/467-4400.

American Astronautical Society, P.O. Box 28130, San Diego, CA 92128. 714/746-4005; 714/487-7560.

American Chemical Society, Microform Program, 1155 Sixteenth St., N.W., Washington, DC 20036. 202/872-4600.

American Concrete Institute, P.O. Box 19150 Redford Station, 22400 W. Seven Mile Rd., Detroit, MI 48219. 313/532-2600.

American Institute of Aeronautics and Astronautics, Inc., 750 Third Ave., New York, NY 10017. 212/867-8300.

American Institute of Physics, 335 East 45th St., New York, NY 10017. 212/661-9404.

American Jewish Periodical Center, Hebrew Union College, 3101 Clifton Ave., Cincinnati, OH 45220. 513/221-1875.

American Library Association, 50 East Huron St., Chicago, IL 60611. 312/944-6780.

American Theological Library Association Board of Microtext, P.O. Box 111, Princeton, NJ 08540. 609/921-8300.

Americana Unlimited, P.O. Box 50447, 1701 North 11th Avenue, Tucson, AZ 85703. 602/792-3453.

Ammons, Bruce and Carol H. Ammons, Perceptual and Motor Skills/ Psychological Reports, Box 9229, Missoula, MT 59807. 406/243-5091.

AMS Press, Inc., 56 East 13th St., New York, NY 10003. 212/777-4700.

Andronicus Publishing Company, Inc., 666 5th Ave., New York, NY 10019. 212/245-8498.

Angus, Gordon, Edinburgh University Press, 22 George Square, Edinburgh EH8 9LF, Scotland. (031) 667-1011.

Antiquarian and Landmarks Society, Inc., 394 Main Street, Hartford, CT 06103. 203/247-8996.

The Architectural Press Ltd., 9 Queen Annes Gate, London SW1H 9BY England. (01) 930-0611.

Archives Canada Microfiches, 395 Wellington Street, Ottawa, Ontario K1A ON3 Canada. 613/995-1300.

Aschenborn, H. J., The Pretoria State Library, P.O. Box 397, Pretoria, South Africa. 48-3920.

Ashby, Peter, Oxford Microform Publications Ltd., Blue Boar Street, Oxford OX1 4EY, England. Oxford 723731.

Association Pour la Conservation et la Reproduction Photographique de la Presse, 4, Rue Louvois, 75002 Paris, France. 742-51-48.

L'Avant-Scène, 27 rue Saint-André-des-Arts, 75006 Paris, France. 325-52-29.

Avedon, Don M., Microfilming Corporation of America, 21 Harristown Rd., Glen Rock, NJ 07452. 201/447-3000.

B

Baker, G. G., Microfilm Association of Great Britain, 1 and 2 Trinity Churchyard, High St., Guilford, Surrey, England. Godalming 6653.

Barlow, D. H., INSPEC, Savoy Place, London WC2R OBL England. (01) 240-1871.

Bartlett, Robert C., Commerce Clearing House, Inc., 4025 W. Peterson Ave., Chicago, IL 60646. 312/CO-7-9010.

Bashore, Melvin L., The Church of Jesus Christ of Latter-Day Saints, Historical Department, East Wing, 50 East North Temple Street, Salt Lake City, UT 84150. 801/531-2745.

Begg, M. A., National Library of Scotland, George IV Bridge, Edinburgh EH1 1EW, Scotland. (031) 226-4531.

Beil, John P., Congressional Information Service, Inc., 7101 Wisconsin Ave., Washington, DC 20014. 301/654-1550.

Bell & Howell Micro Photo Division, Old Mansfield Rd., Wooster, OH 44691. 216/264-6666.

Benson, Maxine, State Historical Society of Colorado, 1300 Broadway, Denver, CO 80203. 303/839-2305.

Benz, I., Microforms International Marketing Corporation, Fairview Park, Elmsford, NY 10523. 914/592-9143.

Berandol Music Limited, 11 St. Joseph St., Toronto, Ontario, M4Y 1J8 Canada. 416/924-8121.

Berger, Robin, Pick Publishing Corporation, 21 West Street, New York, NY 10006. 212/944-5960.

Bernick, Herman C., Library Resources Inc., 425 N. Michigan Ave., Chicago, IL 60611. 312/321-7444.

Bibliothèque Nationale du Québec, Service de microphotographie, 1700, rue Saint-Denis, Montréal, Quebéc, Canada H2X 3K6. 514/670-3470.

Biewen, Robert L., Academic Press, Inc., 111 Fifth Ave., New York, NY 10003. 212/741-6800.

Biosciences Information Service, 2100 Arch St., Philadelphia, PA 19103. 215/LO-8-4016.

Blackwell, Julian, Blackwell Bibliographical Services Limited, P.O. Box 72, Oxford, OX1 2EY England. (0865) 49111 ext. 68.

Blackwell Bibliographical Services Limited, P.O. Box 72, Oxford, OX1 2EY England. (0865) 49111, ext. 68.

Blanchard, Francis, International Labour Office, Publications, CH-1211 Geneva 22, Switzerland. 99-61-11.

Block, I. Edward, SIAM, 33 South 17th Street, Philadelphia, PA 19103. 215/564-2929.

Boni, Albert, Readex Microprint Corp., 101 Fifth Ave., New York, NY 10003. 212/243-3822.

Boni, William F., Readex Microprint Corp., 101 Fifth Ave., New York, NY 10003. 212/243-3822.

Borsodi Victor, Springer-Verlag New York, Inc., 175 Fifth Avenue, New York, NY 10010. 212/673-2660.

Boyd, Allen R., African Imprint Library Services, Guard Hill Rd., Bedford, NY 10506. 914/234-3752.

Boylan, Ray, Center for Research Libraries, 5721 South Cottage Grove, Chicago, II 60637. 312/955-4545.

British Library. Bibliographic Services Division, Store St., London WC1E 7DG England. (01) 636-1544.

Brimelow, Judith M., South Carolina Department of Archives and History, 1430 Senate St., P.O. Box 11, 669, Capitol Station, Columbia, SC 29211. 803/758-5816.

Broadbent, Margaret, The Rockefeller University Press, 1230 York Avenue, New York, NY 10021. 212/360-1278.

Broekhoff, Jan, University of Oregon, College of Health, Physical Education and Recreation, Eugene, OR 97403. 503/686-4117.

Brookhaven Press, 901 26th Street NW, Washington, DC 20037. 202/338-8870.

Brouder, Bernard, Springer-Verlag New York Inc., 175 Fifth Avenue, New York, NY 10010. 212/673-2660.

Brown, Curtis, The Institute of Paper Chemistry, 1043 East South River Street, Appleton, WI 54911. 414/734-9251.

Brown, T. Wistar, IV, Scholarly Resources, Inc., 1508 Pennsylvania Avenue, Wilmington, DE 19806. 302/654-7713.

Browne, S. I., Irish Microforms Ltd., 124 Ranelagh, Dublin 6, Ireland. (01) 961133.

Brownstein, Cy, Microfiche Publications, 440 Park Ave. So., New York, NY 10016. 212/679-3132.

de Bruin, A., Microfiche Foundation, 101 Doelenstraat Delft, The Netherlands. 015-133222 ext. 5677.

Buchanan, William W., The Carrollton Press, 1911 Fort Myer Drive, #905, Arlington, VA 22209. 703/525-5940.

Buchanan, William W., The United States Historical Documents Institute, 1911 Fort Myer Drive, Arlington, VA 22209. 703/525-6035.

Buckett, James, State Historical Society of Wisconsin, Library, 816 State St., Madison, WI 53706. 608/262-9583.

Buckman, Thomas R., The Foundation Center, 888 Seventh Avenue, New York, NY 10019. 212/975-1120.

Budd, Joan, Wildlife Disease Association, P.O. Box 886, Ames, IA 50010. 515/232-1433.

Bueschel, Richard T., Time Share Corporation, Micropublishing, 3 Lebanon St., Hanover, NH 03755. 603/643-3640.

Buffalo and Erie County Historical Society, 25 Nottingham Court, Buffalo, NY 14216. 716/873-9644.

Burke, Frank G., National Historical Publications and Records Commission, National Archives Bldg., Washington, DC 20408. 202/523-3234.

Burn, John A., Unifo Publishers Ltd., P.O. Box 89, White Plains, NY 10602. 914/592-8710.

Burnside, Tom, Helios, Pawlet, VT 05761. 802/325-3360.

Alvina Treut Burrows Institute, Inc., Box 49, Manhasset, NY 11030. 516/869-8457.

Butchywood, Jim, Updata Publications, Inc., 1756 Westwood Blvd., Los Angeles, CA 90024. 213/474-5900.

Butterworths Pty. Ltd., 586 Pacific Hwy. Chatswood N.S.W. 2067 Australia. (02) 412-3444.

C

California State Library, P.O. Box 2037, Sacramento, CA 95809. 916/445-5156.

Campbell, Robert, Oxford Microform Publications Ltd., Blue Boar Street, Oxford OX1 4EY, England. Oxford 723731.

Canadian Library Association, 151 Sparks St., Ottawa, Ontario, Canada K1P 5E3. 613/232-9625.

J. S. Canner & Company, 49-65 Lansdowne St., Boston, MA 02215. 617/261-8600

Caribbean Imprint Library Services, Guard Hill Rd., Bedford, NY 10506. 914/234-3752.

Carrino, Elnora, State University of New York Press, 99 Washington Ave., Albany, NY 12210. 518/474-6050.

Carroll, Walter J., Olympic Media Information, 71 West 23 Street, New York, NY 10010. 212/675-4500.

The Carrollton Press, 1911 Fort Myer Drive, #905, Arlington, VA 22209. 703/525-5940.

The Catholic University of America Press, Inc., 620 Michigan Ave., N.E., Washington, DC 20064. 202/635-5052.

Center for Chinese Research Materials, 1527 New Hampshire Ave., N.W., Washington, DC 20036. 202/387-7172.

Center for Research Libraries, 5721 South Cottage Grove, Chicago, IL 60637. 312/955-4545.

Centner, Léon, Microéditions Hachette, 6 rue Casimir Delavigne-75006 Paris, France. 329-77-41.

Central Asian Research Centre, Ltd. 1B Parkfield St., London, N1 OPR England. (01)226-5371.

The Centre for East Asian Cultural Studies, c/o The Toyo Bunko (Oriental Library), Honkomagome 2-chome, 28-21, Bunkyo-ku Tokyo, 113, Japan. (03)942-0121.

Chadwyck-Healey, Charles, Chadwyck-Healey Ltd., 20 Newmarket Road, Cambridge, England. (0223)311479.

Chadwyck-Healey Ltd., 20 Newmarket Road, Cambridge, England. (0223) 311479.

Chapman & Hall Ltd., Northway, Andover, Hampshire SP105BE England. (0264) 62141.

Charles, Augustine J., Gaylord Bros., Inc., P.O. Box 61, Syracuse, NY 13201. 315/457-5070.

Charrière, Jacques, L'Avant-Scène, 27, rue Saint-André-des-Arts, 75006 Paris, France. 325-52-29.

Chemical Abstracts Service, Ohio State University, Columbus, OH 43210. 614/421-6940.

The Chemical Society, Burlington House, London W1V OBN, England. (01)734-9864.

Chilton Book Company, Radner, PA 19089. 215/687-8200.

Chrisman, Dorothy, Library Microfilms, 737 Loma Verde Ave., Palo Alto, CA 94303. 415/494-1812.

Christiano, David, Meiklejohn Civil Liberties Institute, 1715 Francisco St., Berkeley, CA 94703. 415/848-0599.

The Church of Jesus Christ of Latter-Day Saints, Historical Department, East Wing, 50 East North Temple Street, Salt Lake City, UT 84150. 801/531-2745.

Ciregna, Serge, Paris Publications Inc., 2 Haven Ave., Port Washington, NY 11050. 516/883-4650.

Clearwater Publishing Company, Inc., 75 Rockefeller Plaza, New York, NY 10019. 212/765-0555.

Cohen, David R., Trans-Media, 75 Main St., Dobbs Ferry, NY 10522. 914/693-5956.

Cohen, Herbert C., Information Handling Services, 15 Inverness Way East, Englewood, CO 80150. 303/779-0600.

Cohen, Philip F., Trans-Media, 75 Main St., Dobbs Ferry, NY 10522. 914/693-5956.

Collins, D. F., Microfile Limited, P.O. Box 61328, Marshalltown, 2107, Johannesburg, South Africa. 836-7662.

Colman, Gould P., Cornell University Department of Manuscripts University Archives, John M. Olin Research Library, Ithaca, NY 14850. 607/256-3530.

Commander, J. E., Scolar Press Ltd., 39 Great Russell St., London WC1B 3PH England. (01) 636-1865.

Commander, John E., Mansell Information/Publishing Ltd., 3 Bloomsbury Place, London, WC1A 2QA England. (01)580-6784.

Commerce Clearing House, Inc., 4025 W. Peterson Ave., Chicago, IL 60646. 312/CO-7-9010.

Commonwealth Microfilm Library, 7502 Bath Rd., Mississauga, Ontario, Canada L4T 1L2. 416/677-0697.

Computer Science Press, Inc., 9125 Fall River Lane, Potomac, MD 20854. 301/299-2040.

Congressional Digest Corporation, 3231 P Street N.W., Washington, D.C. 20007. 202/333-7332.

Congressional Information Service, Inc., 7101 Wisconsin Ave., Washington, DC 20014. 301/654-1550.

Congressional Quarterly, 1414 22nd St., N.W., Washington DC 20037. 202/296-6800.

Consumers' Association, 14 Buckingham Street, London WC 2N 6DS England. (01) 839-1222.

Cook, M. Paul, The Michie Company, P.O. Box 57, Charlottesville, VA 22902. 804/295-6171.

Cooper, Harry, National Microfilm Library, 8090 Engineer Road, San Diego, CA 92111. 714/560-8051; 1-800/854-2670.

Copeland, Cheryl, General Microfilm Company, 100 Iman St., Cambridge, MA 02139. 617/864-2820.

Cornell University Department of Manuscripts University Archives, John M. Olin Research Library, Ithaca, NY, 14850. 607/256-3530.

de Corro, Alejandro, IDAL, Información Documental de América Latina, 4824 Ch. Côte des Neiges, Montréal, Qué., Canada H3V 1G4. 514/735-5945.

Coward, Richard, British Library. Bibliographic Services Division, Store St., London WC1E 7DG England. (01) 636-1544.

Cowitt, Philip, Pick Publishing Corporation, 21 West Street, New York, NY 10006. 212/944-5960.

Cox, Gordon L., Americana Unlimited, P.O. Box 50447, 1701 North 11th Avenue, Tucson, AZ 85703. 602/792-3453.

Cox, Nigel S. M., Blackwell Bibliographical Services Limited, P.O. Box 72, Oxford, OX1 2EY England. (0865) 49111, ext. 68.

Crawford, Clifford, Princeton Microfilm Corporation, Alexander Road, Princeton, NJ 08540. 609/452-2066.

Crawford, Franklin D., Princeton Microfilm Corporation, Alexander Road, Princeton, NJ 08540. 609/452-2066.

Crawford, Franklin D., The United States Historical Documents Institute, 1911 Fort Myer Drive, Arlington, VA 22209. 703/525-6035.

Creative Microlibraries, Inc., Box 49, Manhasset, NY 11030. 516/869-8457.

Creps, John E., Jr, Engineering Index, Inc., 345 E. 47th St., New York, NY 10017. 212/644-7600.

Cripe, Helen, Scholarly Resources, Inc., 1508 Pennsylvania Avenue, Wilmington, DE 19806. 302/654-7713.

Crockett, Ethel S., California State Library, P.O. Box 2037, Sacramento, CA 95809. 916/445-5156.

Crone, W. R., Institute of Electrical and Electronics Engineers, 345 E. 47th St., New York, NY 10017. 212/644-7557.

Cruickshank, Ralph, Berandol Music Limited, 11 St. Joseph St., Toronto, Ontario, M4Y 1J8 Canada. 416/924-8121.

Curley, Walter W., Gaylord Bros., Inc., P.O. Box 61, Syracuse, NY 13201. 315/457-5070.

Cuthriell, Robert, Congressional Quarterly, 1414 22nd. St., N.W. Washington, DC 20037. 202/296-6800.

D

Dakota Graphics, Inc., 9655 W. Colfax Ave., Denver, CO 80215. 303/237-0408.

Dartmouth College Library, Baker Library, Hanover, NH 03755. 603/646-2235.

Dashfield, D.C., Her Majesty's Stationery Office, Atlantic House, Holborn Viaduct, London EC1P 1BN England. (01) 248-9876.

Data Courier, Inc., 620 South Fifth Street, Louisville, KY 40202. 502/582-4111.

Dataflow Systems, Inc., 7758 Wisconsin Ave., Bethesda, MD 20014. 301/654-9133.

Davidson, John McI., Edinburgh University Press, 22 George Square, Edinburgh EH8 9LF, Scotland. (031) 667-1011.

Davis, D. Farrell, Greenwood Press, 51 Riverside Ave., Westport, CT 06880. 203/226-3571.

Davis, Robert, National Design Center, Inc., 425 E. 53rd Street, New York, NY. 212/MU-8-5200.

Wm. Dawson & Sons Ltd., Cannon House, Folkestone, Kent CT19 5EE England. Folkestone 57421.

Deahl, Thomas F., Microdoc, 815 Carpenter Lane, Philadelphia, PA 19119. 215/848-4545.

DeAngelis, John, Dakota Graphics, Inc., 9655 W. Colfax Ave., Denver, CO 80215. 303/237-0408.

Debrégeas-Laurenie, Geneviève, Institut d'Ethnologie. Muséum National d'Histoire Naturelle, Palais de Chaillot, place du Trocadéro 75116 Paris, 75116 Paris, France. 553-82-15.

De Gier, Nico, Excerpta Medica, 305 Keizersgracht, Amsterdam, The Netherlands. (020) 644-38.

Delisle, Georges, Archives Canada Microfiches, 395 Wellington Street, Ottawa, Ontario, K1A ON3 Canada. 613/995-1300.

DeStephen, Anthony, Princeton Microfilm Corporation, Alexander Road, Princeton, NJ 08540. 609/452-2066.

Detmers, Arthur C., Buffalo and Erie County Historical Society, 25 Nottingham Court, Buffalo, NY 14216. 716/873-9644.

Diaz, Albert, Brookhaven Press, 901 26th Street NW, Washington, DC 20037. 202/338-8870.

Disclosure Incorporated, 4827 Rugby Avenue, Bethesda, MD 20014. 301/931-0100.

Dodeman, Jacques, France Expansion, 336-340 rue Saint Honore 75001 Paris, France. 260-32-09.

Doudnikoff, B. Dataflow Systems, Inc., 7758 Wisconsin Ave., Bethesda, MD 20014. 301/654-9133.

Dresia, David R., American Institute of Physics, 335 East 45th St., New York, NY 10017. 212/661-9404.

Duncan, J. Douglas, Juta & Company Limited, Mercury Crescent, Welton 7790, South Africa. 71-1181.

Duncan, John E., Mansell Information/Publishing Ltd., 3 Bloomsbury Place, London, WC1A 2QA England. (01) 580-6784.

Dundas, Robert G., Springer-Verlag New York Inc., 175 Fifth Avenue, New York, NY 10010. 212/673-2660.

The Dunlap Society, Visual Documentation Program, Box 297, Essex, NY 12936. 518/963-7373.

E

Eaton, June S., Mansell Information/Publishing Ltd., 3 Bloomsbury Place London, WC1A 2QA England. (01) 580-6784.

Ede, J. R., Public Record Office, Chancery Lane, London WC2 1LR, England. (01) 405-0741.

Edinburgh University Press, 22 George Square, Edinburgh EH8 9LF, Scotland. (031) 667-1011.

Educational Information Services, Inc., Air Rights Bldg., P.O. Box 5826, Washington, DC 20014. 301/770-6440.

Educational Resources Information Center, Washington, DC 20208. 202/254-5555.

Educational Testing Service, Princeton, NJ 08540. 609/921-9000.

Edward, Charles V. R., Commerce Clearing House, Inc., 4025 W. Peterson Ave., Chicago, IL 60646. 312/CO-7-9010.

Eichenberger, Herbert, Inter Documentation Company AG, Postrasse 14, Zug, Switzerland. 42-214974.

Elias, A. W., Biosciences Information Service, 2100 Arch St., Philadelphia, PA 19103. 215/LO-8-4016.

Ellegood, Donald R., University of Washington Press, Seattle, WA 98195. 206/543-4050.

Ellen, Gina, Updata Publications, Inc., 1756 Westwood Blvd., Los Angeles, CA 90024. 213/474-5900.

Ellis, Donald J., Microfilming Corporation of America, 21 Harristown Rd., Glen Rock, NJ 07452. 201/447-3000.

Elsevier Sequoia S. A., Avenue de la Gare 50, P.O. Box 851, 1001 Lausanne, Switzerland. (021) 207381.

Elsmark, Iran M.C.S., International Labour Office, Publications, CH-1211, Geneva 22, Switzerland. 99-61-11.

Embryo Publishers, 17 Woodside Place, Glascow C3, Scotland. (041) 332-1066.

Emerson, William R., Franklin D. Roosevelt Library, Albany Post Rd., Hyde Park, NY 12538. 914/229-8114.

Emmert, Helen, Pick Publishing Corporation, 21 West Street, New York, NY 10006. 212/944-5960.

Engels, Vel, Johnson Associates Inc., P.O. Box 1017, 321 Greenwich Ave., Greenwich, CT 06830. 203/661-7602.

Engfield, Roy H., National Library of Canada, 395 Welllington St., Ottawa, Canada K1A ON4. 613/995-9481.

Engineering Index, Inc., 345 E. 47th St., New York, NY 10017. 212/644-7600.

Environment Information Center, 292 Madison Avenue, New York, NY 10017. 212/949-9494.

EP Microform Limited, Bradford Rd., East Ardsley, Wakefield, Yorkshire, WF3 2JN England. Wakefield (0924) 823971.

Epstein, Howard M., Facts on File, Inc., 119 West 57th Street, New York, NY 10019. 212/CO-5-2011.

Eustis, John P., II, General Microfilm Company, 100 Iman St., Cambridge, MA 02139. 617/864-2820.

Everitt, Alastair, Harvester Press Ltd., 2 Stanford Terrace, Hassocks, North Brighton, Sussex, England; Microform Department, 17 Ship Street, Brighton, Sussex, England. Brighton 5532 & 4378.

Excerpta Medica, 305 Keizersgracht, Amsterdam, The Netherlands. (020) 644-38.

F

Facts on File, Inc., 119 West 57th Street, New York, NY 10019. 212/CO-5-2011.

Fairchild Microfilms, Visuals Division, Fairchild Publications, Inc., 7 East 12th St., New York, NY 10003. 212/741-4067.

Farnsley, Charles, Lost Cause Press, 750-56 Starks Bldg., Louisville, KY 40202. 502/584-8404.

Farnsley, Nancy, Lost Cause Press, 750-56 Starks Bldg., Louisville, KY 40202. 502/584-8404.

Farrant, D. H., Microfile Limited, P.O. Box 61328, Marshalltown, 2107, Johannesburg, South Africa. 836-7662.

Ferguson, Thomas, New University Press, Inc., 520 N. Michigan Ave., Chicago, IL 60611. 312/828-0420.

Ferster, Paul, Research Publications, Inc., 12 Lunar Dr., Woodbridge, CT 06525. 203/397-2600.

Filby, P. William, Maryland Historical Society, 201 W. Monument St., Baltimore, MD 20201. 301/685-3750.

The Financial Times, Bracken House, Cannon St., London EC4P 4BY England. (01) 248-8000.

Fisher, Lincoln, Law Reprints, Inc., 37 West 20th Street, New York, NY 10011. 212/242-5358.

Fitzsimmons, Joseph J., University Microfilms International, 300 North Zeeb Road, Ann Arbor, MI 48106. 313/761-4700.

Flesher, Brian, Greenwood Press, 51 Riverside Ave., Westport, CT 06880. 203/226-3571.

Fondation Nationale des Sciences Politiques, 27 rue Saint-Guillaume, 75341 Paris Cedex 07, France. 260-39-60.

The Foundation Center, 888 Seventh Avenue, New York, NY 10019. 212/975-1120.

France-Expansion. 336-340 rue Saint Honore 75001 Paris, France. 260-32-09.

Frazer, Claude R., Princeton Datafilm, Inc., P.O. Box 231, Princeton Jct., NJ 08550. 609/779-1630.

Freedman, Samuel B., Research Publications, Inc., 12 Lunar Dr., Woodbridge, CT 06525. 203/397-2600.

G

Gannett, E. K., Institute of Electrical and Electronics Engineers, 345 E. 47th St., New York, NY 10017. 212/644-7557.

Gardner, W. H., H. Pordes, 529B, Finchley Rd., London, NW3 7BH England. (01) 435-9878.

Gatenby, Joan, Library Microfilms, 737 Loma Verde Ave., Palo Alto, CA 94303. 415/494-1812.

Gaylord Bros., Inc., P.O. Box 61, Syracuse, NY 13201. 315/457-5070.

General Microfilm Company, 100 Iman St., Cambridge, MA 02139. 617/864 2820.

Geoghegan, Margery, Central Asian Research Centre, Ltd., 1B Parkfield St., London, N1 0PR England. (01) 226-5371.

George, C. S., The Institute for Advanced Studies of World Religions, 5001 Melville Memorial Library, SUNY-Stony Brook, New York, NY 11794. 516/246-8362.

Georgia Institute of Technology, Georgia Tech Libraries, Atlanta, GA 30332. 404/894-4510.

Gibson, Robert, Micromedia Limited, Box 502, Station S, Toronto, Canada M5M 4L8. 416/489-8016.

Gilbert, J. G., The Michie Company, P.O. Box 57, Charlottesville, VA 22902. 804/295-6171.

Gilchriese, John D., Americana Unlimited, P.O. Box 50447, 1701 North 11th Avenue, Tucson, AZ 85703. 602/792-3453.

Gille, Dominique, Micro-Urba, BP 241, 13605 Aix en Provence, France. (42) 27-68-37.

Gilligan, Jim, University Microfilms International, 300 North Zeeb Road, Ann Arbor, MI 48106. 313/761-4700.

Ginger, Ann Fagan, Meiklejohn Civil Liberties Institute, 1715 Francisco St., Berkeley, CA 94703. 415/848-0599.

Ginsberg, Norman, National Design Center, Inc., 425 E. 53rd Street, New York, NY 10022. 212/MU-8-5200.

Godfrey Memorial Library, Middletown, CT 06457. 203/DI-6-4375.

Goetze, H., Springer-Verlag New York Inc., 175 Fifth Avenue, New York, NY 10010. 212/673-2660.

Golding, Nigel, MacLean-Hunter Limited Microform Services, 481 University Ave., Toronto, Ontario, Canada M5W 1A7. 416/595-1811.

Goldman, Peter, Consumers' Association, 14 Buckingham Street, London WC2N 6DS England. (01) 839-1222.

Goldspiel, Steven, Disclosure Incorporated, 4827 Rugby Avenue, Bethesda, MD 20014. 301/931-0100.

Goldstein, Howard, Congressional Information Service, Inc., 7101 Wisconsin Ave., Washington, DC 20014. 301/654-1550.

Golzen, G., The Architectural Press Ltd., 9 Queen Annes Gate, London SW1H 9BY England. (01) 930-0611.

Goode, Marian E., The Catholic University of America Press, Inc., 620 Michigan Ave., N.E., Washington, DC 20064. 202/635-5052.

Gordon, Martin, Gordon and Breach Science Publishers Ltd., 41/42 William IV Street, London WC2 England. (01) 836-5125.

Gordon and Breach Science Publishers Ltd., 41/42 William IV Street, London WC2 England. (01) 836-5125.

Gordon and Breach Science Publishers Inc., 1 Park Avenue, New York, NY 10016. 212/689-0360.

Grant, Henry, Facts on File, Inc., 119 West 57th Street, New York, NY 10019. 212/CO-5-2011.

Gray, Edward, Microforms International Marketing Corporation, Fairview Park, Elmsford, NY 10523. 914/592-9143.

Gray, Susan B., Micrographics II, Rt. 7, Box 258G, Charlottesville, VA 22901. 804/296-0596.

Greenway, Helen, University Microfilms International, 300 North Zeeb Road, Ann Arbor, MI 48106. 313/761-4700.

Greenwood Press, 51 Riverside Ave., Westport, CT 06880. 203/226-3571.

Gregg, Newton K., Gregg Music Sources, P.O. Box 1459, Rohnert Park, CA 94928. 707/526-3161; 707/632-5387.

Gregg Music Sources, P.O. Box 1459, Rohnert Park, CA 94928. 707/526-3161; 707/632-5387.

Grenga, Kathy, The Southern Baptist Convention Historical Commission, 127 Ninth Ave., North, Nashville, TN 37234. 615/251-2660.

Grice, Maureen, Clearwater Publishing Company, Inc., 1995 Broadway, Room 401, New York, NY 10023. 212/873-2100.

Grice, Maureen, International Microform Distribution Service, 1995 Broadway, Room 401, New York, NY 10023. 212/873-2100.

Griffen, David, United Nations, Publications Section, Room LX 2300, New York, NY 10017. 212/754-1234.

Grills, Caroline M., American Chemical Society, Microform Program, 155 Sixteenth St. N.W., Washington, DC 20036. 202/872-4600.

Grossman, Bernd, Springer-Verlag New York Inc., 175 Fifth Avenue, New York, NY 10010. 212/673-2660.

Gstalder, Herbert W., KTO Microform Division, Route 100, Millwood, NY 10546. 914/762-2200.

Walter de Gruyter, Inc., 3 Westchester Plaza, Elmsford, NY 10523. 914/592-5890.

Guiart, Jean, Institute d'Ethnologie. Muséum National d'Histoire Naturelle. Palais de Chaillot, place du Trocadéro 75116, Paris, France. 533-82-15.

Gunn, Mike, World Microfilms Publications Ltd., 62 Queen's Grove, London NW8 6ER, England. (01) 586-3092.

Gurr, Graham, 3M Company, Library Systems, Box 33600, St. Paul, MN 55133. 612/733-1186.

H

Hafgren, Bjorn, United Nations, Publications Section, Room LX 2300, New York, NY 10017. 212/754-1234.

Hagelstein, Robert, Greenwood Press, 51 Riverside Ave., Westport, CT 06880. 203/226-3571.

Hair, Hugh B., SIAM, 33 South 17th Street, Philadelphia, PA 19103. 215/564-2929.

Hajicek, Robert F., West Publishing Company, 50 W. Kellog, P.O. Box 3526, St. Paul, MN 55165. 612/228-2971.

Haldi, John, Andronicus Publishing Company, Inc., 666 5th Ave., New York, NY 10019. 212/245-8498.

Hall, Charles H., United Nations, Publications Section, Room LX 2300, New York, NY 10017. 212/754-1234.

Halprin, Steve, Information Design Inc., 3247 Middlefield Rd., Menlo Park, CA 94025. 415/369-2962.

Hamilton, Mickey, Hoover Institution Press, Stanford University, Stanford, CA 94305. 415/321-2300 ext. 3373.

Harland, G., Wm. Dawson & Sons Ltd., Cannon House, Folkestone, Kent CT19 5EE England. Folkestone 57421.

Harvard University Press, 79 Garden Street, Cambridge, MA 02138. 617/495-2600.

Harvester Press Ltd., 2 Stanford Terrace, Hassocks, North Brighton, Sussex, England; Microform Department, 17 Ship Street, Brighton, Sussex, England. Brighton 5532 & 4378.

Hastings, J., The Architectural Press Ltd., 9 Queen Annes Gate, London SW1H 9BY England. (01) 930-0611.

Hattery, Lowell H., Lomond Publications, P.O. Box 56, Mt. Airy, MD 21771. 301/829-1633.

Hawkins, William, Service International de Microfilms, 9 rue du Commandant Riviere, Paris 8, France. 359-16-31.

William S. Hein & Co., Inc. Micro-Film Division, 1285 Main St., Buffalo, NY 14209. 716/882-2600.

Heinzer-Fähndrich, Roswitha, Inter Documentation Company AG, Postrasse 14, Zug, Switzerland. 42-214974.

Helios, Pawlet, VT 05761. 802/325-3360.

Helmstadter, Daniel C., Scholarly Resources, Inc., 1508 Pennsylvania Avenue, Wilmington, DE 19806. 302/654-7713.

Her Majesty's Stationery Office, Atlantic House, Holborn Viaduct, London EC1P 1BN England. (01) 248-9876.

Heyden, Gunter, Heyden & Son Limited, Spectrum House, Alderton Crescent, London NW4 3XX, England. (01) 202-5333.

Heyden & Son Limited, Spectrum House, Alderton Crescent, London NW4 3XX, England. (01) 202-5333.

Heynen, Jeffrey, Congressional Information Service, Inc., 7101 Wisconsin Ave., Washington, DC 20014. 301/654-1550.

Hickson, Wanda, University of Oregon, College of Health, Physical Education and Recreation, Eugene, OR 97403. 503/686-4117.

Hill Monastic Manuscript Library, Bush Center, St. John's University, Collegeville, MN 56321. 612/363-3514.

Historical Society of Pennsylvania, 1300 Locust Street, Philadelphia, PA 19107. 215/732-6200.

Hixon, Philip E., Disclosure Incorporated, 4827 Rugby Avenue, Bethesda, MD 20014. 301/931-0100.

Hodder, John, University Microfilms Limited, 18 Bedford Row, London WC1R 4EJ, England. (01) 242-9485.

Hoffman, Ernest, Americana Unlimited, P.O. Box 50447, 1701 North 11th Avenue, Tucson, AZ 85703. 602/792-3453.

Hoffman, Harry, Ingram Book Company, 347 Redwood Drive, Nashville, TN 37217. 615/889-3000.

Holbert, Sue E., Minnesota Historical Society, 1500 Mississippi Street, St. Paul, MN 55101. 612/296-6980.

Holland, Mark, Harvester Press Ltd., 2 Stanford Terrace, Hassocks, North Brighton, Sussex, England; Microform Department, 17 Ship Street, Brighton, Sussex, England. Brighton 5532 & 4378.

Holman, Eloise, SIAM, 33 South 17th Street, Philadelphia, PA 19103. 215/564-2929.

Hootman, Ron, National Microfilm Library, 8090 Engineer Road, San Diego, CA 92111. 714/560-8051; 1-800/854-2670.

Hoover, Charles, Educational Resources Information Center, Washington, DC 20208. 202/254-5555.

Hoover Institution Press, Stanford University, Stanford, CA 94305. 415/321-2300 ext. 3373.

Horder, Alan, The National Reprographic Centre for documentation, The Hatfield Polytechnic, Endymion Road Annexe, Hatfield, Herts AL10 8AM England. Hatfield 66144.

Horwitz, Karl, Microfilming Corporation of America, 21 Harristown Rd., Glen Rock, NJ 07452. 201/447-3000.

Houser, Anthony, University Publications of America, Inc., 5630 Connecticut Avenue, Washington, DC 20015. 202/362-6201.

Human Relations Area File, P.O. Box 2054 Yale Station, 755 Prospect St. New Haven, CT 06520. 203/777-2334.

Hur, Robert C., Congressional Quarterly, 1414 22nd St. N.W., Washington, DC 20037. 202/296-6800.

Hyatt, Ott H., University of Washington Press, Seattle, WA 98195. 206/543-4050.

I

IDAL, Información Documental de América Latina, 4824 Ch. Côte des Neiges, Montréal, Qué., Canada H3V 1G4. 514/735-5945.

Ikuta, Shigeru, The Centre for East Asian Cultural Studies, c/o The Toyo Bunko (Oriental Library), Honkomagome 2-chome, 28-21, Bunkyo-ku Tokyo, 113, Japan. (03) 942-0121.

Illinois State Historical Library, Old State Capitol, Springfield, IL 62706. 217/782-4836.

Immigration History Research Center, University of Minnesota, 826 Berry Street, St. Paul, MN 55114. 612/373-5581.

Informações, Microformas e Sistemas S/A, Rua Mateus Grou, 57, São Paulo, Brazil. 280-4759; 853-6680.

Information Design Inc., 3247 Middlefield Rd., Menlo Park, CA 94025. 415/369-2962.

Information Handling Services, 15 Inverness Way East, Englewood, CO 80150. 303/779-0600.

Information Resources Press, 2100 M Street, N.W., Suite 316, Washington, DC 20037. 202/293-2605.

Ingram Book Company, 347 Reedwood Drive, Nashville, TN 37217. 615/889-3000.

INSPEC, Savoy Place, London WC2R 0BL England. (01) 240-1871.

Institut d'Ethnologie. Muséum National d'Histoire Naturelle. Palais de Chaillot, place du Trocadéro 75116. Paris, France. 553-82-15.

The Institute for Advanced Studies of World Religions, 5001 Melville Memorial Library, SUNY-Stony Brook, New York, NY 11794. 516/246-8362.

Institute of Electrical and Electronics Engineers, 345 E. 47th St., New York, NY 10017. Information 212/644-7557; orders, 201/981-0060.

The Institute of Paper Chemistry, 1043 East South River Street, Appleton, WI 54911. 414/734-9251.

The Institute of Physics, Publishing Division, Techno House, Redcliffe Way, Bristol BS1 6NX, England. 0272-297481.

Inter Documentation Company AG. Postrasse 14, Zug, Switzerland. 42-214974.

International Labour Office, Publications, CH-1211 Geneva 22, Switzerland. 99-61-11.

International Microform Distribution Service, 75 Rockefeller Plaza, New York, NY 10019. 212/765-0556.

International Microform Distribution Service, 231 Hollyberry Trail, Willowdale, Ontario, Canada M2H 2P3. 416/494-6143.

International Trade Centre, Palais des Nations, CH-1211, Genève 10, Switzerland. 31-12-55.

Irish Microforms Ltd., 124 Ranelagh, Dublin 6, Ireland. (01) 961133.

J

Jackson, Norma C., The Dunlap Society, Visual Documentation Program, Box 297, Essex, NY 12936. 518/963-7373.

Jacobs, H., American Astronautical Society, P.O. Box 28130, San Diego, CA 92128. 714/746-4005; 714/487-7560.

Jacobs, H., Univelt Inc., P.O. Box 28130, San Diego, CA 92128. 714/746-4005 or 714/487-7560.

Jambois, Frank, Northern Micrographics, P.O. Box 1653, LaCrosse, WI 54601. 608/782-4180.

Jansen, Arnold A.J., Excerpta Medica, 305 Keizersgracht, Amsterdam, The Netherlands. (020) 644-38.

Jeanneret, Marsh, University of Toronto Press, St. George Campus, Toronto, Ont. M5S 1A6 Canada. 416/978-2239.

Jefferson, Celia, Tuskegee Institute, Division of Behavioral Science Research, Tuskegee Institute, AL 36088. 205/727-8575.

Jenkins, Myra Ellen, New Mexico State Records Center and Archives, 404 Montezuma, Sante Fe, NM 87501. 505/827-2321.

Jewish Chronicle Limited, 25 Furnival St., London, EC4A 1JT, England. (01) 405-9252.

Jewitt, Clement, Blackwell Bibliographical Services Limited, P.O. Box 72, Oxford, OX1 2EY England. (0865) 49111, ext. 68.

Johnson, Cathy, TV Guide, Radnor, PA 19088. 215/688-7400.

Johnson, Herbert M., Johnson Associates Inc., P.O. Box 1017, 321 Greenwich Ave., Greenwich, CT 06830. 203/661-7602.

Johnson Associates Inc., P.O. Box 1017, 321 Greenwich Avenue, Greenwich, CT 06830. 203/661-7602.

Johnston, Catherine, Mansell Information/Publishing Ltd., 3 Bloomsbury Place, London, WC1A 2QA England. (01) 580-6784.

Jones, Daniel S., NewsBank, Inc., P.O. Box 10047, 741 Main Street, Stamford, CT 06904. 203/357-8894.

Jones, Robert B., Ohio Historical Society, Interstate 71 & 17th Avenue, Columbus, OH 43211. 614/466-2060.

Judge, Colin, Oxford Publishing Company, 5 Lewis Close, Risington, Headington, Oxford, England. (0865) 66215.

Juta & Company Limited, Mercury Crescent, Welton 7790; P.O. Box 123, Kenwyn 7790, South Africa. 71-1181.

K

Kane, Lucile M., Minnesota Historical Society, 1500 Mississippi Street, St. Paul, MN 55101. 612/296-6980.

Keil, Carl, The New York Times Information Bank, 229 West 43rd St., New York, NY 10036. 212/556-1111.

Kemplin, Martha, Chilton Book Company, Radner, PA 19089. 215/687-8200.

Kennedy, H. E., Biosciences Information Service, 2100 Arch St., Philadelphia, PA 19103. 215/LO-8-4016.

Kesaris, Paul, University Publications of America, Inc., 5630 Connecticut Avenue, Washington, DC 20015. 202/362-6201.

King, Elmer S., The Library of Congress, Photoduplication Service, 10 First Street, S.E., Washington, DC 20540. 202/426-5652.

Kirsch, William, The Foundation Center, 888 Seventh Avenue, New York, NY 10019. 212/975-1120.

Knappman, Edward, Facts on File, Inc., 119 West 57th Street, New York, NY 10019. 212/CO-5-2011.

Koeltzsch, J., Georg Olms Verlag GmbH, Hagentorwall 6-7, D-3200 Hildesheim, West Germany. (051 21) 3-70-07.

Kollegger, James, Environment Information Center, 292 Madison Avenue, New York, NY 10017. 212/949-9494.

Koszyk, Kurt, Mikrofilmarchiv der Deutschsprachigen Presse E.V., D. 4600 Dortmund, Hansaplatz, West Germany. 542-23216.

Kramer, Sheldon, University Microfilms International, 300 North Zeeb Road, Ann Arbor, MI 48106. 313/761-4700.

Krayenbrink, G., Wm. Dawson & Sons Ltd., Cannon House, Folkestone, Kent CT19 5EE England. Folkestone 57421.

Kretschmann, Gisela, Schnase Microfilm Systems, 120 Brown Rd., Scarsdale, NY 10583. 914/725-1284.

KTO Microform Division, Route 100, Millwood, NY 10546. 914/762-2200.

Kurz, Peter, Somerset House, 417 Maitland Avenue, Teaneck, NJ 07666. 201/833-1795.

Kurzig, Carol M., The Foundation Center, 888 Seventh Avenue, New York, NY 10019. 212/975-1120.

Kyte, Colin, Newspaper Archive Developments Limited, 16 Westcote Road, Reading, RG3 2DF, England. (0734) 583247.

L

LaBarre, C. A., United States Government Printing Office, Washington, DC 20402. 202/275-3345.

Lagace, Robert O., Human Relations Area File, P.O. Box 2054 Yale Station, 755 Prospect St., New Haven, CT 06520. 203/777-2334.

LaHood, Charles G., Jr., The Library of Congress, Photoduplication Service, 10 First Street, S.E., Washington, DC 20540. 202/426-5652.

Laing, W. Scott, United Nations, Publications Section, Room LX2300, New York, NY 10017. 212/754-1234.

LaMotte, Victor, New University Press, Inc., 520 N. Michigan Ave., Chicago, IL 60611. 312/828-0420.

Langer, Howard, Facts on File, Inc., 119 West 57th Street, New York, NY 10019. 212/CO-5-2011.

Law Reprints, Inc., 37 West 20th Street, New York, NY 10011. 212/242-5358.

Lawrence, Lewis H., Lawrence Newspapers, Inc., P.O. Box 1015, Fuquay-Varina, NC 27526. 919/552-5178.

Lawrence Newspapers, Inc., P.O. Box 1015, Fuquay-Varina, NC 27526. 919/552-5178

H. R. Lawrence Publications, 308 Sackett Building, University Park, PA 16802. 814/865-9535.

Lawson, Ann, Meiklejohn Civil Liberties Institute, 1715 Francisco St., Berkeley, CA 94703. 415/848-0599.

Lebowitz, Marshall, J. S. Canner & Company, 49-65 Lansdowne St., Boston, MA 02215. 617/261-8600.

Lee, B. C. E., Her Majesty's Stationery Office, Atlantic House, Holborn Viaduct, London EC1P 1BN England. (01) 248-9876.

Lee, Edward M., Information Handling Services, 15 Inverness Way East, Englewood, CO 80150. 303/779-0600.

Leeds Polytechnic School of Librarianship, 28 Park Palce, Leeds LS1 2SY, United Kingdom. 0532-456696.

Lehanka, Charles, American Institute of Physics, 335 East 45th St., New York, NY 10017. 212/661-9404.

Leinbach, Donald, University Music Editions, P.O. Box 192, Fort George Station, NY 10040. 212/569-5393/5340.

Leroi-Gourhan, André, Institut d'Ethnologie. Muséum National d'Histoire Naturelle. Palais de Chaillot, place du Trocadéro 75116, Paris, France. 553-82-15.

Lexander, George M., General Microfilm Company, 100 Iman St., Cambridge, MA 02139. 617/864-2820.

Library Microfilms, 737 Loma Verde Ave., Palo Alto, CA 94303. 415/494-1812.

The Library of Congress, Photoduplication Service, 10 First Street, S.E., Washington, DC 20540. 202/426-5652.

Library Resources Inc., 425 Michigan Ave., Chicago, IL 60611. 312/321-7444.

Lindahl, Charles, Sibley Music Library Microform Service, 44 Swan St., Rochester, NY 14604. 716/275-3018.

Litto, Fredric M., Informções, Microformas e Sistemas S/A, Rua Mateus Grou, 57, São Paulo, Brazil. 280-4759; 853-6680.

Lofthouse, J. S., EP Microform Limited, Bradford Rd., East Ardsley, Wakefield, Yorkshire, WF3 2JN England. Wakefield (0924) 823971.

Lomond Publications, P.O. Box 56, Mt. Airy, MD 21771. 301/829-1633.

Loscalzo, Anne, Trans-Media, 75 Main St., Dobbs Ferry, NY 10522. 914/693-5956.

Lost Cause Press, 750-56 Starks Bldg., Louisville, KY 40202. 502/584-8404.

Lowitz, Barbara, University Publications of America, Inc., 5630 Connecticut Avenue, Washington, DC 20015. 202/362-6201.

Lowry, Isabel Barrett, The Dunlap Society, Visual Documentation Program, Box 297, Essex, NY 12936. 518/963-7373.

Lucas, Lydia A., Minnesota Historical Society, 1500 Mississippi Street, St. Paul, MN 55101. 612/296-6980.

Lunn, Anita P., Ohio Historical Society, Interstate 71 & 17th Avenue, Columbus, OH 43211. 614/466-2060.

Luther, Frederic, The Frederic Luther Company, 2803 East 56th Street, Indianapolis, IN 46220. 317/253-3446.

The Frederic Luther Company, 2803 East 56th Street, Indianapolis, IN 46220. 317/253-3446.

M

McClenahan, W. S., The Institute of Paper Chemistry, 1043 East South River Street, Appleton, WI 54911. 414/734-9251.

McFarland, Howard, American Concrete Institute, P.O. Box 19150 Redford Station, 22400 W. Seven Mile Rd., Detroit, MI 48219. 313/532-2600.

McGowan, Richard J., KTO Microform Division, Route 100, Millwood, NY 10546. 914/762-2200.

McGill, Raymond D., James T. White and Company, 1700 State Highway Three, Clifton, NJ 07013. 201/773-9300.

McGreevy, James S., The Carrollton Press, 1911 Fort Myer Drive, #905, Arlington, VA 22209. 703/525-5940.

McLaren, Duncan, McLaren Micropublishing, P.O. Box 972, Station F, Toronto, Canada M4Y 2N9. 416/461-1627.

McLaren Micropublishing, P.O. Box 972, Station F, Toronto, Canada M4Y 2N9. 416/461-1627.

MacLean-Hunter Limited Microfilm Services, 481 University Ave., Toronto, Ont., Canada M5W 1A7. 416/595-1811.

Malcom, J. B., Dataflow Sytems, Inc., 7758 Wisconsin Ave., Bethesda, MD 20014. 301/654-9133.

Maltese, G., Microfiche Publications, 440 Park Ave. So., New York, NY 10016. 212/679-3132.

Mandel, Milton, Research Publications, Inc., 12 Lunar Dr., Woodbridge, CT 06525. 203/397-2600.

Mangouni, Norman, Scholars' Facsimiles & Reprints, P.O. Box 344, Delmar, NY 12054. 518/439-6146.

Mangouni, Norman, State University of New York Press, 99 Washington Ave., Albany, NY 12210. 518/474-6050.

Mann, Lorne C., Commonwealth Microfilm Library, 7502 Bath Rd., Mississauga, Ontario, Canada L4T 1L2. 416/677-0697.

Mansell Information/Publishing Ltd., 3 Bloomsbury Place, London, WC1A 2QA England. (01) 580-6784.

MARC Applied Research Company, P.O. Box 40035, Washington, DC 20016. 301/840-1480.

Marchisotto, R., Biosciences Information Service, 2100 Arch St., Philadelphia, PA 19103. 215/LO-8-4016.

Mariella, Raymond P., American Chemical Society, Microform Program, 1155 Sixteenth St., N.W., Washington, DC 20036. 202/872-4600.

Marken, John C., Bell & Howell Micro Photo Division, Old Mansfield Rd., Wooster, OH 44691. 216/264-6666.

Maryland Historical Society, 201 W. Monument St., Baltimore, MD 20201. 301/685-3750.

Massachusetts Historical Society, 1154 Bolylston St., Boston, MA 02215. 617/536-1608.

Massey, Don W., Micrographics II, Rt. 7, Box 258G, Charlottesville, VA 22901. 804/296-0596.

May, Lynn E., Jr., The Southern Baptist Convention Historical Commission, 127 Ninth Ave., North, Nashville, TN 37234. 615/251-2660.

Meckler, Alan Marshall, Microform Review, Inc., 520 Riverside Ave., P.O. Box 405 Saugatuck Station, Westport, CT 06880. 203/226-6967.

Meiklejohn Civil Liberties Institute, 1715 Francisco St., Berkeley, CA 94703. 415/848-0599.

Menzies, Merrilyn, Maclean-Hunter Limited Microfilm Services, 481 University Ave., Toronto, Ont., Canada M5W 1A7. 416/595-1811.

Mertens, E., Georg Olms Verlag GmbH, Hagentorwall 6-7, D-3200 Hildesheim, West Germany. (05121) 3-70-07.

Mevers, Frank C., New Hampshire Historical Society, Thirty Park Street, Concord, NH 03301. 603/226-3381.

Michaels, Edward, Allerton Press, Inc., 150 Fifth Ave., New York, NY 10011. 212/924-3950.

Michaud, Jean-Pierre, Microéditions Hachette, 6, rue Casimir Delevigne-75006 Paris, France. 329-77-41.

The Michie Company, P.O.Box 57, Charlottesville, VA 22902. 804/295-6171.

Micro-Comfax Inc., 925 Kranzel Drive, Camp Hill, PA 17011. 717/761-5030.

Microdoc, 815 Carpenter Lane, Philadelphia, PA 19119. 215/848-4545.

Microéditions Hachette, 6, rue Casimir Delavigne-75006 Paris, France. 329-77-41.

Microfiche Foundation, 101 Doelenstraat Delft, The Netherlands. 015-133222 ext. 5677.

Microfiche Publications, 440 Park Ave. So., New York, NY 10016. 212/679-3132.

Microfile Limited, P.O. Box 61328, Marshalltown, 2107, Johannesburg, South Africa. 836-7662.

Microfilm Association of Great Britain, 1 and 2 Trinity Churchyard, High St., Guildford, Surrey, England. Godalming 6653.

Microfilm Center, Inc., P.O. Box 45436, Dallas, TX 75235. 214/358-5231.

Microfilm Corporation of Pennsylvania, 141 South Highland Ave., Pittsburgh, PA 15206. 412/661-9280.

Microfilming Corporation of America, 21 Harristown Rd., Glen Rock, NJ 07452. 201/447-3000.

Microform Review, Inc., 520 Riverside Ave., P.O. Box 405 Saugatuck Station, Westport, CT 06880. 203/226-6967.

Microforms International Marketing Corporation, Fariview Park, Elmsford, NY 10523. 914/592-9143.

Micrographic Publication Service, 5455 Wilshire Blvd., Suite 1009, Los Angeles, CA 90036. 213/938-5274.

Micrographics II, Rt. 7 Box 258G, Charlottesville, VA 22901. 804/296-0596.

Microinfo Ltd., P.O. Box 3, Alton, Hampshire, GU 34 1EF England. Alton 84300.

Micrologue, Inc., 2010 Curtis St., Denver, CO 80205. 303/892-9344.

Micromedia Limited, Box 502, Station S, Toronto, Canada M5M 4L8. 416/489-8016.

Micro-Urba, BP 241 13605 Aix en Provence, France. (42) 27-68-37.

Miklas, K. K., Readex Microprint Corp., 101 Fifth Ave., New York, NY 10003. 212/243-3822.

Mikrofilmarchiv der Deutschsprachigen Presse E.V., D. 4600 Dortmund, Hansaplatz, West Germany. 542-23216.

Mikropress GmbH, D-53 Bonn, Baunscheidt str. 17 West Germany. 231688.

Milligan, Stuart, Sibley Music Library Microform Service, 44 Swan St., Rochester, NY 14604. 716/275-3018.

Mindata Ltd., 32 The Mall, London W5 3TW England. (01) 579-1679.

Minnesota Historical Society, 1500 Mississippi Street, St. Paul, MN 55101. 612/296-6980.

Mitura, Anthony M., KTO Microform Division, Route 100, Millwood, NY 10546. 914/762-2200.

Monod, N., International Labour Office, Publications, CH-1211 Geneva 22, Switzerland. 99-61-11.

Moore, Mary Ellen, Yale University Library, Publications Office, New Haven, CT 06520. 203/436-8335.

Morgan, J. P., Her Majesty's Stationery Office, Atlantic House, Holborn Viaduct, London EC1P 1BN England. (01) 248-9876.

Morison, David L., Central Asian Research Centre, Ltd., 1B Parkfield St., London, N1 0PR England. (01) 226-5371.

Morris, R. A., Society of Automotive Engineers, Inc., 400 Commonwealth Dr., Warrendale, PA 15096. 412/776-4841.

Morton, Bonnie L., William S. Hein & Co., Inc., Micro-Film Division, 1285 Main St., Buffalo, NY 14209. 716/882-2600.

Moscato, John, University Publications of America, Inc., 5630 Connecticut Avenue, Washington, DC 20015. 202/362-6201.

Mulvihill, Stephen J., Information Handling Services, 15 Inverness Way East, Englewood, CO 80150. 303/779-0600.

Munro, Craig, University of Queensland Press Microform Division, P.O. Box 42, St. Lucia, Qld. 4067 Australia. 3706291 (Brisbane).

Murphy, Brian P., Harvard University Press, 79 Garden Street, Cambridge, MA 02138. 617/495-2600.

Murphy, Brower, MARC Applied Research Company, P.O. Box 40035, Washington, DC 20016. 301/840-1480.

Murray, Hallam, Scolar Press Ltd., 39 Great Russell St., London WC1B 3PH England. (01) 636-1865.

N

Nash, Mary M., Mary Nash Information Services, 188 Dagmar Ave., Vanier, Ontario, K1L 5T2 Canada. 613/745-5112.

Mary Nash Information Services, 188 Dagmar Ave., Vanier, Ontario, K1L 5T2 Canada. 613/745-5112.

National Design Center, 425 E. 53rd Street, New York, NY 10022.
212/MU8-5200.

National Historical Publications and Records Commission, National Archives
Bldg., Washington, DC 20408. 202/523-3234.

National Library of Australia, Canberra ACT 2600, Australia. (062) 621-111.

National Library of Canada, 395 Wellington St., Ottawa, Canada K1A ON4.
613/995-9481.

National Library of Scotland, George IV Bridge, Edinburgh EH1 1EW,
Scotland. (031) 226-4531.

National Microfilm Library, 8090 Engineer Road, San Diego, CA 92111. 714/
560-8051; 1-800/854-2670.

National Micrographics Association, 8728 Colesville Rd., Silver Spring, MD
20910. 301/587-8444.

The National Reprographic Centre for Documentation, The Hatfield
Polytechnic, Endymion Road Annexe, Hatfield, Herts AL10 8AM England.
Hatfield 66144.

National Technical Information Service, 5285 Port Royal Road, Springfield,
VA 22161. 703/557-4630.

Nelson, Louis B., Information Handling Services, 15 Inverness Way East,
Englewood, CO 80150. 303/779-0600.

New Hampshire Historical Society, Thirty Park Street, Concord, NH 03301.
603/226-3381.

New Mexico State Records Center and Archives, 404 Montezuma, Santa Fe,
NM 87501. 505/827-2321.

New University Press, Inc., 520 N. Michigan Ave., Chicago, IL 60611.
312/828-0420.

New York Law Journal, 258 Broadway, New York, NY 10007. 212/964-9400.

New York Public Library, Photographic Service, Fifth Avenue & 42nd Street,
New York, NY 10018. 212/790-6262.

The New York Times Information Bank, 229 West 43rd St., New York, NY
10036. 212/556-1111.

Newman, Edwin S., Trans-Media, 75 Main St., Dobbs Ferry, NY 10522.
914/693-5956.

NewsBank, Inc., P.O. Box 10047, 741 Main Street, Stamford, CT 06904.
203/357-8894.

Newspaper Archive Developments Limited, 16 Westcote Road, Reading,
RG3 2DF, England. (0734) 583247.

Nikola, Sotir, Microforms International Marketing Corporation, Fairview Park,
Elmsford, NY 10523. 914/592-9143.

Nitta, Yuji, Yushodo Film Publications, Ltd., 29 Saneicho, Shinjuku-ku, Tokyo,
Japan. 03-357-1411.

Norman, Douglas, University Microfilms International, 300 North Zeeb Rd.,
Ann Arbor, MI 48106. 313/761-4700.

Northern Micrographics, P.O. Box 1653, LaCrosse, WI 54601. 608/782-4180.

Jeffrey Norton Publishers, Inc., 145 East 49th Street, New York, NY 10017.
212/753-1783.

O

Ohio Historical Society, Interstate 71 & 17th Avenue, Columbus, OH 43211. 614/466-2060.
Olms, Georg W., Georg Olms Verlag GmbH, Hagentorwall 6-7, D-3200 Hildesheim, West Germany. (05121) 3-70-07.
Georg Olms Verlag GmbH, Hagentorwall 6-7, D-3200 Hildesheim, West Germany. (05121) 3-70-07.
Olson, Robert C., Microfilming Corporation of America, 21 Harristown Rd., Glen Rock, NJ 07452. 201/447-3000.
Olympic Media Information, 71 West 23 Street, New York, NY 10010. 212/675-4500.
Omniwest Corporation, 3322 So. 3rd East, Salt Lake City, UT 84115. 801/486-3563.
O'Neil, Stephen, New University Press, Inc., 520 N. Michigan Ave., Chicago, IL 60611. 312/828-0420.
Oxford Microform Publications Ltd., Blue Boar Street, Oxford OX1 4EY, England. Oxford 723731.
Oxford Publishing Company, 5 Lewis Close, Risington, Headington, Oxford, England. (0865) 66215.
Oxford University Press, 200 Madison Ave., New York, NY 10016. 212/679-7300.

P

Page, Leslie A., Wildlife Disease Association, P.O. Box 886, Ames, IA 50010. 515/232-1433.
Paine, F. Ward, Information Design Inc., 3247 Middlefield Rd., Menlo Park, CA 94025. 415/369-2962.
Palmer, Patricia J., The Stanford University Libraries, Special Collections, Stanford, CA 94305. 415/321-2300.
Paris Publications Inc., 2 Haven Ave., Port Washington, NY 11050. 516/883-4650.
Parker, Peter J., Historical Society of Pennsylvania, 1300 Locust Street, Philadelphia, PA 19107. 215/732-6200.
Parrish, D. W., The Michie Company, P.O. Box 57, Charlottesville, VA 22902. 804/295-6171.
Pavlakis, Christopher, University Music Editions, P.O. Box 129, Fort George Station, NY 10040. 212/569-5393/5340.
Payne, Lorna, Newspaper Archive Developments Limited, 16 Westcote Road, Reading, RG3 2DF, England. (0734) 583247.
Pearce, Dwain, Bell & Howell Micro Photo Division, Old Mansfield Rd., Wooster, OH 44691. 216/264-6666.
Peck, Barbara J., Predicasts, Inc., 11001 Cedar Ave., Cleveland, OH 44106. 216/795-3000.

Pederson, C. I., The Institute of Physics, Publishing Division Techno House, Redcliffe Way, Bristol BS1 6NX, England. 0272-297481.

Perceptual and Motor Skills/Psychological Reports, Box 9229, Missoula, MT 59807. 406/243-5091.

Perry, D., Her Majesty's Stationery Office, Atlantic House, Holborn Viaduct, London EC1P 1BN England. (01) 248-9876.

Peters, Wilhelm, Mikropress GmbH, D-53 Bonn, Baunscheidtstr. 17 West Germany. 231688.

Phelps, Edward, Canadian Library Association, 151 Sparks St., Ottawa, Ontario, Canada K1P 5E3. 613/232-9625.

Philipson, Morris, The University of Chicago Press, 5801 Ellis Ave., Chicago, IL 60637. 312/753-2564.

Pick, Franz, Pick Publishing Corporation, 21 West Street, New York, NY 10006. 212/944-5960.

Pick Publishing Corporation, 21 West Street, New York, NY 10006. 212/944-5960.

Pickett, Reg, Harvester Press Ltd., 2 Stanford Terrace, Hassocks, North Brighton, Sussex, England; Microform Department, 17 Ship Street, Brighton, Sussex, England. Brighton 5532 & 4378.

Plante, Julian G., Hill Monastic Manuscript Library, Bush Center, St. John's University, Collegeville, MN 56321. 612/363-3514.

Platt, Carol A., Micrographic Publication Service, 5455 Wilshire Blvd., Suite 1009, Los Angeles, CA 90036. 213/938-5274.

Plenum Publishing Corporation, 227 West 17th Street, New York, NY 10011. 212/255-0713.

H. Pordes, 529B, Finchley Rd., London, NW3 7BH England. (01) 435-9878.

Post, Doris, Godfrey Memorial Library, Middletown, CT 06457. 203/DI-6-4375.

Precedent Publishing, Inc., 520 North Michigan Avenue, Chicago, IL 60611. 312/828-0420.

Predicasts, Inc., 11001 Cedar Ave., Cleveland, OH 44106. 216/795-3000.

Presbyterian Historical Society, 425 Lombard St., Philadelphia, PA 19147. 215/MA-7-1852.

Preston, James L., Scholarly Resources, Inc., 1508 Pennsylvania Avenue, Wilmington, DE 19806. 302/654-7713.

The Pretoria State Library, P.O. Box 397, Pretoria, South Africa. 48-3920.

Prevel, James J., Educational Information Services, Inc., Air Rights Bldg., P.O. Box 5826, Washington, DC 20014. 301/770-6440.

Priest, Lyle, Information Design Inc., 3247 Middlefield Rd., Menlo Park, CA 94025. 415/369-2962.

Princeton Datafilm, Inc., P.O. Box 231, Princeton Jct., NJ 08550. 609/799-1630.

Princeton Microfilm Corporation, Alexander Road, Princeton, NJ 08540. 609/452-2066.

Public Record Office, Ruskin Avenue, Kew, Richmond, Surrey TW9 4DU, England; Chancery Lane, London WC2 1LR, England. (01) 876-3444; (01) 405-0741.

Publications Orientalists de France, 4 rue de Lille, 75007 Paris, France. 260-67-05.

Puckett, Sam B., Information Design Inc., 3247 Middlefield Rd., Menlo Park, CA 94025. 415/369-2962.

Pullen, Beverly, The Financial Times, Bracken house, Cannon St., London EC4P 4BY England. (01) 248-8000.

Puttmann, Rick, Micrologue, Inc., 2010 Curtis St., Denver, CO 80205. 303/ 892-9344.

R

Readex Microprint Corp., 101 Fifth Ave., New York, NY 10003. 212/243-3822.

Regan, J. M., The Architectural Press Ltd., 9 Queen Annes Gate, London SW1H 9BY England. (01) 930-0611.

Reno, Edward A., Microfilming Corporation of America, 21 Harristown Rd., Glen Rock, NJ 07452. 201/447-3000.

Research Publications, Inc., 12 Lunar Dr., Woodbridge, CT 06525. 203/397-2600.

Rhea, D. L., Microfilm Center, Inc., P.O. Box 45436, Dallas, TX 75235. 214/358-5231.

Rice, Stevens, University Microfilms International, 300 North Zeeb Road, Ann Arbor, MI 48106. 313/761-4700.

Roberts, Graham, Georgia Institute of Technology, Georgia Tech Libraries, Atlanta, GA 30332. 404/894-4510.

Robinson, A. Gram, Congressional Digest Corporation, 3231 P Street N.W., Washington, DC 20007. 202/333-7332.

Robinson, T. N., III, Congessional Digest Corporation, 3231 P Street N.W., Washington, DC 20007. 202/333-7332.

Robson, David, Newspaper Archive Developments Limited, 16 Westcote Road, Reading, RG3 2DF, England. (0734) 583247.

The Rockefeller University Press, 1230 York Avenue, New York, NY 10021. 212/360-1278.

Franklin D. Roosevelt Library, Albany Post Road, Hyde Park, NY 12538. 914/229-8114.

Rosen, Lewis J., Clearwater Publishing Company, Inc., 231 Hollyberry Trail, Willowdale, Ontario, Canada M2H 2P3. 416/494-6143.

Rosen, Lewis J., International Microforms Distribution Service, 231 Hollyberry Trail, Willowdale, Ontario, Canada M2H 2P3. 416/494-6143.

Rosen, Pamela, Educational Testing Service, Princeton, NJ 08540. 609/921-9000.

Rosenthal, Arthur J., Harvard University Press, 79 Garden Street, Cambridge, MA 02138. 617/495-2600.

Ross, Norman Z., Clearwater Publishing Company, Inc., 1995 Broadway, Room 401, New York, NY 10023. 212/873-2100.

Ross, Warren D., Gaylord Bros., Inc., P.O. Box 61, Syracuse, NY 13201.
315/457-5070.
Rothman, Fred B., Fred B. Rothman & Co., 57 Leuning St., South
Hackensack, NJ 07606. 201/489-4646.
Rothman, Paul A., Fred B. Rothman & Co., 57 Leuning St., South
Hackensack, NJ 07606. 201/489-4646.
Fred B. Rothman & Co., 57 Leuning St., South Hackensack, NJ 07606.
201/489-4646.
Rust, Harvey G., Microfilm Center, Inc., P.O. Box 45436, Dallas, TX 75235.
214/358-5231.

S

Saadus, Ann, Hoover Institution Press, Stanford University, Stanford, CA
94305. 415/321-2300.
Sadler, I. G., The Institute of Physics, Publishing Division Techno House,
Redcliffe Way, Bristol BS1 6NX, England. 0272-297481.
Salender, Bruce, Jeffrey Norton Publishers, Inc., 145 East 49th Street, New
York, NY 10017. 212/753-1783.
Saunders, Joy, Heyden & Son Limited, Spectrum House, Alderton Crescent,
London NW4 3XX, England. (01) 202-5333.
Savard, Réjean, Bibliothèque Nationale du Québec, Service de
microphotographie, 1700, rue Saint-Denis, Montréal, Quebéc, Canada H2X
3K6. 514/670-3470.
Sawyer, Dave, Microfilm Center, Inc., P.O. Box 45436, Dallas, TX 75235.
214/358-5231.
Scarpulla, Joseph, AMS Press, Inc., 56 East 13th St., New York, NY 10003.
212/777-4700.
Schechter, Allen, Commerce Clearing House, Inc., 4025 W. Peterson Ave.,
Chicago, IL 60646. 312/CO-7-9010.
Scheffler, Eckart A., Walter de Gruyter, Inc., 3 Westchester Plaza, Elmsford,
NY 10523. 914/592-5890.
Schierenberg, Dieter, Schierenberg, Dieter B.V., Amsteldijk 44, Amsterdam,
The Netherlands. (020) 769280.
Schierenberg, Dieter B.V., Amsteldijk 44, Amsterdam, The Netherlands.
(020) 769280.
Schnase, Annemarie, Schnase Microfilm Systems, 120 Brown Rd.,
Scarsdale, NY 10583. 914/725-1284.
Schnase Microfilm Systems, 120 Brown Rd., Scarsdale, NY 10583.
914/725-1284.
Schoenherr, Douglas, Archives Canada Microfiches, 395 Wellington Street,
Ottawa, Ontario, K1A ON3 Canada. 613/995-1300.
Scholarly Resources, Inc., 1508 Pennsylvania Avenue, Wilmington, DE
19806. 302/654-7713.

Scholars' Facsimiles & Reprints, P.O. Box 344, Delmar, NY 12504.
518/439-6146.

Schuman, Joan B., The Williams & Wilkins Co., 428 E. Preston St., Baltimore,
MD 21202. 301/528-4249.

Schwanke, Kathy, Perceptual and Motor Skills/Psychological Reports, Box
9229, Missoula, MT 59807. 406/243-5091.

Sclar, Herbert, Updata Publications, Inc., 1756 Westwood Blvd., Los Angeles,
CA 90024. 213/474-5900.

Scolar Press Ltd., 39 Great Russell St., London WC1B 3PH England.
(01) 636-1865.

Seeberg-Elverfeldt, Roland, Mikrofilmarchiv der Deutschsprachigen Presse
E.V., D. 4600 Dortmund, Hansaplatz, West Germany. 542-23216.

Selwyn, Roy, Microinfo Ltd., P.O. Box 3, Alton, Hampshire, GU34 1EF
England. Alton 84300.

Service International de Microfilms, 9 Rue du Commandant Riviere, Paris 8,
France. 359-16-31.

Sexton, Marie, National Library of Australia, Canberra ACT 2600, Australia.
(062) 621-111.

Sheldon, Anne, Oxford Microform Publications Ltd., Blue Boar Street, Oxford
OX1 4EY, England. Oxford 723731.

Shelley, Fred, National Historical Publications and Records Commission,
National Archives Bldg., Washington, DC 20408. 202/523-3234.

Shen, C. T., The Institute for Advanced Studies of World Religions, 5001
Melville Memorial Library, SUNY-Stony Brook, New York, NY 11794.
516/246-8362.

Sheppard, Roger and Judith, Trigon Press, 117 Kent House Road,
Beckenham Kent BR3 1JJ, England. (01) 778-0534.

Shields, John E., Congressional Digest Corporation, 3231 P Street N.W.,
Washington, DC 20007. 202/333-7332.

Short, Jeanne, Microform Review, Inc., 520 Riverside Ave., P.O. Box 405
Saugatuck Station, Westport, CT 06880. 203/226-6967.

Shurlock, E. M., Barry Shurlock & Co. (Publishers) Ltd., 174 Stockbridge
Road, Winchester Hants, 5022 6RW England. (0962) 67030.

Barry Shurlock & Co. (Publishers) Ltd., 174 Stockbridge Road, Winchester
Hants, 5022 6RW England. (0962) 67030.

SIAM, 33 South 17th Street, Philadelphia, PA 19103. 215/564-2929.

Sibley Music Library Microform Service, 44 Swan St., Rochester, NY 14604.
716/275-3018.

Sidor, Linda, Johnson Associates Inc., P.O. Box 1017, 321 Greenwich Ave.,
Greenwich, CT 06830. 203/661-7602.

Sieffert, Simone, Publications Orientalistes de France, 4, rue de Lille, 75007
Paris, France. 260-67-05.

Silware, Ralph, Disclosure Incorporated, 4827 Rugby Avenue, Bethesda, MD
20014. 301/931-0100.

Simon Fraser University, Office of the University Librarian, Burnaby 2, British
Columbia, Canada. 604/291-3261.

Simpson, Robert, University Microfilms Limited, 18 Bedford Row, London WC1R 4EJ, England. (01) 242-9485.

Slosson, Theodore C., Jr., Princeton Datafilm, Inc., P.O. Box 231, Princeton Jct., NJ 08550. 609/799-1630.

Smith, J. R., Biosciences Information Service, 2100 Arch St., Philadelphia, PA 19103. 215/LO-8-4016.

Smith, Lester W., Buffalo and Erie County Historical Society, 25 Nottingham Court, Buffalo, NY 14216. 716/873-9644.

Snyder, Robert N., Disclosure Incorporated, 7827 Rugby Avenue, Bethesda, MD 20014. 301/931-0100.

Society of Automotive Engineers, Inc., 400 Commonwealth Dr., Warrendale, PA 15096. 412/776-4841.

Society of Exploration Geophysicists, 3707 E. 51 St., Tulsa, OK 74135. 918/743-1365.

Somerset House, 417 Maitland Avenue, Teaneck, NJ 07666. 201/833-1795.

Somerville, Romaine, Maryland Historical Society, 201 W. Monument St., Baltimore, MD 20201. 301/685-3750.

South Carolina Department of Archives and History, 1430 Senate Street, P.O. Box 11, 669, Capitol Station, Columbia, SC 29211. 803/758-5816.

The Southern Baptist Convention Historical Commission, 127 Ninth Ave., North, Nashville, TN 37234. 615/251-2660.

Southern Illinois University Press, P.O. Box 3697, Carbondale, IL 62901. 618/453-2281-2.

Spence, Paul, Illinois State Historical Library, Old State Capitol, Springfield, IL 62706. 217/782-4836.

Spencer, John, The National Reprographic Centre for documentation, The Hatfield Polytechnic, Endymion Road Annexe, Hatfield, Herts AL10 8AM England. Hatfield 66144.

Spiers, John, Harvester Press Ltd., 2 Stanford Terrace, Hassocks, North Brighton, Sussex, England; Microform Department, 17 Ship Street, Brighton, Sussex, England. Brighton 5532 & 4378.

Springer, Kathy, American Association for the Advancement of Science, 1515 Massachusetts Ave., N.W., Washington, DC 20005. 202/467-4400.

Springer-Verlag New York Inc., 175 Fifth Avenue, New York, NY 10010. 212/673-2660.

The Stanford University Libraries, Special Collections, Stanford, CA 94305. 415/321-2300.

Starbird, Carolyn, National Technical Information Service, 5285 Port Royal Road, Springfield, VA 22161. 703/557-4630.

State Historical Society of Colorado, 1300 Broadway, Denver, CO 80203. 303/839-2305.

State Historical Society of Wisconsin, Library, 816 State St., Madison, WI 53706. 608/262-9583.

State University of New York Press, 99 Washington Ave., Albany, NY 12210. 518/474-6050.

Stern, Barrie, Excerpta Medica, 305 Keizersgracht, Amsterdam, The Netherlands. (020) 644-38.

Steve, George T., Pick Publishing Corporation, 21 West Street, New York, NY 10006. 212/944-5960.

Stinchcomb, Susan, American Association for the Advancement of Science, 1515 Massachusetts Ave., N.W., Washington, DC 20005. 202/467-4400.

Stine, R. R., Dataflow Systems, Inc., 7758 Wisconsin Ave., Bethesda, MD 20014. 301/654-9133.

Strothman, Wendy J., The University of Chicago Press, 5801 Ellis Ave., Chicago, IL 60637. 312/753-2564.

Sung, Carolyn Hoover, The Library of Congress, Photoduplication Service, 10 First Street, S.E., Washington, DC 20540. 202/426-5652.

Surrency, Erwin C., Temple University School of Law, Charles Klein Library, 1715 N. Broad St., Philadelphia, PA 19122. 215/787-7891.

Sussman, Gerald, Oxford University Press, 200 Madison Ave., New York, NY 10016. 212/679-7300.

Svobodny, Dolly, Alvina Treut Burrows Institute, Inc., Box 49, Manhasset, NY 11030. 516/869-8457.

Svobodny, Dolly, Creative Microlibraries, Inc., Box 49, Manhasset, NY 11030. 516/869-8457.

Swets & Zeitlinger B.V., Heereweg 347b, Lisse, The Netherlands. 02521-19113.

T

Taylor, James N., Time Share Corporation, Micropublishing, 3 Lebanon St., Hanover, NH 03755. 603/643-3640.

Taylor and Francis Ltd., 10-14 Macklin St., London WC2B 5NF, England. (01) 405-2237/9.

Teague, S. J., Microfilm Association of Great Britain, 1 and 2 Trinity Churchyard, High St. Guildford, Surrey, England. Godalming 6653.

Temple University School of Law, Charles Klein Library, 1715 N. Broad St., Philadelphia, PA 19122. 215/787-7891.

Thiriet, Françoise, Publications Orientalistes de France, 4, rue de Lille, 75007 Paris, France. 260-67-05. ,

Thomas, Peter, Consumers' Association, 14 Buckingham Street, London WC2N 6DS England. (01) 839-1222.

Thompson, Frank, University of Queensland Press Microform Division, P.O. Box 42, St. Lucia, Qld., 4067 Australia. 3706291 (Brisbane).

3M Company, Library Systems, Box 33600, St. Paul, MN 55133. 612/733-1186.

Time Share Corporation, Micropublishing, 3 Lebanon St., Hanover, NH 03755. 603/643-3640.

Tisdale, Mary, The Carrollton Press, 1911 Fort Myer Drive, #905, Arlington, VA 22209. 703/525-5940.

Tonks, A. Ronald, The Southern Baptist Convention Historical Commission, 127 Ninth Ave., North, Nashville, TN 37234. 615/251-2660.

Trans-Media, 75 Main St., Dobbs Ferry, NY 10522. 914/693-5956.

Trigon Press, 117 Kent House Road, Beckenham Kent BR3 1JJ, England. (01) 778-0534.

Turnbull, Archie, Edinburgh University Press, 22 George Square, Edinburgh EH8 9LF, Scotland. (031) 667-1011.

Tuskegee Institute, Division of Behavioral Science Research, Tuskegee Institute, AL 36088. 205/727-8575.

TV Guide, Radnor, PA 19088. 215/688-7400.

U

Unifo Publishers Ltd., P.O. Box 89, White Plains, NY 10602. 914/592-8710.

United Nations, Publications Section, Room LX 2300, New York, NY 10017. 212/754-1234.

United States Government Printing Office, Washington, DC 20402. 202/275-3345.

The United States Historical Documents Institute, 1911 Fort Myer Drive, Arlington, VA 22209. 703/525-6035.

U.S. National Archives and Records Services, Publications Sales Branch, Washington, DC 20408. 202/523-3181.

Univelt inc., P.O. Box 28130, San Diego, CA 92128. 714/746-4005 or 714/487-7560.

University Microfilms International, 300 North Zeeb Road, Ann Arbor, MI 48106. 313/761-4700.

University Microfilms Limited, 18 Bedford Row, London WC1R 4EJ, England. (01) 242-9485.

University Music Editions, P.O. Box 192, Fort George Station, NY 10040. 212/569-5393/5340.

The University of Chicago Press, 5801 Ellis Ave., Chicago, IL 60637. 312/753-2564.

University of Iowa, Libraries, Iowa City, IA 52242. 319/353-4450.

University of Oregon, College of Health, Physical Education and Recreation, Eugene, OR 97403. 503/686-4117.

University of Queensland Press Microform Division, P.O. Box 42, St. Lucia, Qld., 4067 Australia. 3706291 (Brisbane).

University of Toronto Press, St. George Campus, Toronto, Ont. M5S 1A6 Canada. 416/978-2239.

University of Washington Press, Seattle, WA 98195. 206/543-4050.

University Publications of America, Inc., 5630 Connecticut Avenue, Washington, DC 20015. 202/362-6201.

Updata Publications, Inc., 1756 Westwood Blvd., Los Angeles, CA 90024. 213/474-5900.

V

Valentine, Inge, Springer-Verlag New York Inc., 175 Fifth Avenue, New York, NY 10010. 212/673-2660.

Valentine, Wilbur, U.S. National Archives and Records Service, Publications Sales Branch, Washington, DC 20408. 202/523-3181.

Van Der Lee, Corrie, Princeton Microfilm Corproation, Alexander Road, Princeton, NJ 08540. 609/452-2066.

Van Leeuwen, Willem, Excerpta Medica, 305 Keizersgracht, Amsterdam, The Netherlands. (020) 644-38.

Van Meter, Michael, American Association for the Advancement of Science, 1515 Massachusetts Ave., N.W., Washington, DC 20005. 202/467-4400.

Veaner, Allen B., Microform Review, Inc., 520 Riverside Ave., P.O. Box 405, Saugatuck Station, Westport, CT 06880. 203/226-6967.

Vecoli, Rudolph J., Immigration History Research Center, University of Minnesota, 826 Berry Street, St. Paul, MN 55114. 612/373-5581.

Verlag Dokumentation, Publishers, P.O. Box 711009, Pössenbacherstr. 2, 8000 München 71, Federal Republic of Germany. (089) 798901.

Veyette, John H., Jr., Engineering Index, Inc., 345 E. 47th St., New York, NY 10017. 212/644-7600.

Vieli, Lelio, Inter Documentation Company AG, Postrasse 14, Zug, Switzerland. 42-214974.

Von Knorring, H. J., Chapman & Hall Ltd., Northway, Andover, Hampshire SP105BE England. (0264) 62141.

W

Wall, Paul L., Tuskegee Institute, Division of Behavioral Science Research, Tuskegee Institute, AL 36088. 205/727-8575.

Walsh, John J., Microform Review, Inc., 520 Riverside Ave., P.O. Box 405 Saugatuck Station, Westport, CT 06880. 203/226-6967.

Ward, Dean, Dakota Graphics, Inc., 9655 W. Colfax Ave., Denver, CO 80215. 303/237-0408.

Ward, Dianne E., Americana Unlimited, P.O. Box 50447, 1701 North 11th Avenue, Tucson, AZ 85703. 602/792-3453.

Watanabe, Ruth, Sibley Music Library Microform Service, 44 Swan St., Rochester, NY 14604. 716/275-3018.

Watterson, Hermine M., Andronicus Publishing Company, Inc., 666 5th Ave., New York, NY 10019. 212/245-8498.

Webster, Richard C., Aesthetic, Reconstructive, and Facial Plastic Surgery, 16 Prescott St., Brookline, MA 02146. 617/566-2050.

Weinberg, M., Jewish Chronicle Limited, 25 Furnival Street, London,EC4A 1JT, England. (01) 405-9252.

Weir, Carl, Princeton Microfilm Corporation, Alexander Road, Princeton, NJ 08540. 609/452-2066.

West Publishing Company, 50 W. Kellogg, P.O. Box 3526, St. Paul, MN 55165. 612/228-2971.

J. Whitaker & Sons, Ltd., 12 Dyott Street, London, WC1, England. (01) 637-1105.

White, Bob, Microfilm Center, Inc., P.O. Box 45436, Dallas, TX 75235. 214/358-5231.

White, Howard S., American Library Association, 50 East Huron St., Chicago, IL 60611. 312/944-6780.

White, William H., James T. White and Company, 1700 State Highway Three, Clifton, NJ 07013. 201/773-9300.

James T. White and Company, 1700 State Highway Three, Clifton, NJ 07013. 201/773-9300.

Whitney, Thos. D., Library Microfilms, 737 Loma Verde Ave., Palo Alto, CA 94303. 415/494-1812.

Whitney, Wm. D., Library Microfilms, 737 Loma Verde Ave., Palo Alto, CA 94303. 415/494-1812.

Wilcox, Maud, Harvard University Press, 79 Garden Street, Cambridge, MA 02138. 617/495-2600.

Wildlife Disease Association, P.O. Box 886, Ames, IA 50010. 515/232-1433.

Wiley-Interscience Journals, John Wiley & Sons, Inc., 605 Third Ave., New York, NY 10016. 212/867-9800.

Willard, Charles, American Theological Library Association Board of Microtext, P.O. Box III, Princeton, NJ 08540. 609/921-8300.

Williams, Bernard J. S., The National Reprographic Centre for documentation, The Hatfield Polytechnic, Endymion Road Annexe, Hatfield, Herts AL10 8AM England. Hatfield 66144.

Williams, Ivor A., The Chemical Society, Burlington House, London W1V OBN, England. (01) 734-9864.

Williams, Lyndsay, Chapman & Hall Ltd., Northway, Andover, Hampshire SP105BE England. (0264) 62141.

Williams, Peter, Heyden & Son Limited, Spectrum House, Alderton Crescent, London NW4 3XX, England. (01) 202-5333.

The Williams & Wilkins Co., 428 E. Preston St., Baltimore, MD 21202. 301/528-4249.

Windscheffel, Brian, Oxford Microform Publications Ltd., Blue Boar Street, Oxford OX1 4EY, England. Oxford 723731.

Winkler, William G., Wildlife Disease Association, P.O. Box 886, Ames, IA 50010. 515/232-1433.

Wittman, Allan, Wiley-Interscience Journals, John Wiley & Sons, Inc., 605 Third Ave., New York, NY 10016. 212/867-9800.

Wood, C. J., Butterworths Pty. Ltd., 586 Pacific Hwy. Chatswood N.S.W. 2067 Australia. (02) 412-3444.

Wolff, Jo Ann, Updata Publications, Inc., 1756 Westwood Blvd., Los Angeles, CA 90024. 213/474-5900.

Women's History Research Center, 2325 Oak St., Berkeley, CA 94708. 415/548-1770.

World Microfilms Publications Ltd., 62 Queen's Grove, London NW8 6ER, England. (01) 586-3092.

XYZ

X, Laura, Women's History Research Center, 2325 Oak St., Berkeley, CA 94708. 415/548-1770.

Yale University Library, Publications Office, New Haven, CT 06520. 203/436-8335.

Yokoyama, Katsuyuki, Yushodo Film Publications, Ltd., 29 Saneicho, Shinjuku-ku, Tokyo, Japan. 03-357-1411.

Younger, William E., The Library of Congress, Photoduplication Service, 10 First Street, S.E., Washington, DC 20540. 202/426-5652.

Yu, Ping-kuen, Center for Chinese Research Materials, 1527 New Hampshire Ave., N.W., Washington, DC 20036. 202/387-7172.

Yushodo, Film Publications, Ltd., 29 Saneicho, Shinjuku, Tokyo, Japan. 03-357-1411.

Zafren, Herbert, American Jewish Periodical Center, Hebrew Union College, 3101 Clifton Ave., Cincinnati, OH 45220. 513/221-1875.

Zandvliet, Dr. J., Microfiche Foundation, 101 Doelenstraat Delft, The Netherlands. 015-133222 ext. 5677.

Zentz, Dale H., Scholarly Resources, Inc., 1508 Pennsylvania Avenue, Wilmington, DE 19806. 302/654-7713.

Zeskey, Russell H., Bell & Howell Micro Photo Division, Old Mansfield Rd., Wooster, OH 44691. 216/264-6666.

INDEX TO ADVERTISERS